CHIEF EXECUTIVE TO
CHIEF JUSTICE

CHIEF EXECUTIVE TO CHIEF JUSTICE

Taft betwixt the White House and Supreme Court

LEWIS L. GOULD

UNIVERSITY PRESS OF KANSAS

© 2014 by the University Press of Kansas
All rights reserved

Published by the University Press of Kansas (Lawrence, Kansas 66045), which was
organized by the Kansas Board of Regents and is operated and funded by Emporia
State University, Fort Hays State University, Kansas State University, Pittsburg State
University, the University of Kansas, and Wichita State University

Library of Congress Cataloging-in-Publication Data

Gould, Lewis L.
Chief executive to chief justice : Taft betwixt the White House
and Supreme Court / Lewis L. Gould.
pages cm
Includes bibliographical references and index.
ISBN 978-0-7006-2001-2 (cloth : alk. paper)
1. Taft, William H. (William Howard), 1857–1930. 2. Presidents—United
States—Biography. 3. United States—Politics and government—1913–1921.
I. Title.
E762.G68 2014
973.91′2092—dc23
[B]
2014020688

British Library Cataloguing-in-Publication Data is available.

Printed in the United States of America

10 9 8 7 6 5 4 3 2 1

The paper used in this publication is recycled and contains 30 percent postconsumer
waste. It is acid free and meets the minimum requirements of the American National
Standard for Permanence of Paper for Printed Library Materials Z39.48–1992.

CONTENTS

ACKNOWLEDGMENTS

Many people helped me write this book about William Howard Taft. The staff of the Perry-Castaneda Library at the University of Texas at Austin facilitated my use of the William Howard Taft Papers on microfilm over the course of many years. Clarence and Geri Lasby provided warm hospitality when I returned to Austin for follow-up research in 2013. They have been vital friends for almost half a century. I also want to acknowledge the kindness and support that H. Wayne Morgan extended to me when I first came as a young scholar to the University of Texas in the late 1960s. He was a fine scholar of the Gilded Age and a wonderful teacher.

Kristie Miller of Washington, D.C., helped me renew connections with the Library of Congress that had lapsed for two decades, during an important visit there in November 2013. Her enthusiasm for manuscript research stimulated my own memories of that process and enabled me to accomplish a great deal in a short time.

At Monmouth College, Richard Sayre, director of the Hewes Library, and his talented staff made it possible for me to use the services of the interlibrary loan program to secure needed reels of the Taft Papers in the concluding phase of the project. In my daily life, Mary Lou Pease provided vital assistance with getting me places and keeping me together

Laura Kalman gave the manuscript a thorough reading that tightened the prose and addressed many important substantive issues. Simon and Stacy Cordery sustained me during the transition from

Austin to Monmouth in more fruitful ways than I can enumerate. Stacy also read the manuscript and added her timely suggestions for improvement and clarity.

This book was the first I have written over the past four decades without the encouragement and wise counsel of Karen Gould. It reminded me how much I depended on her affection and support. Dedicating this work to her memory will, I hope, indicate how much I miss all of her presence in my life.

Lewis L. Gould
Monmouth, Illinois
January 2014

CHIEF EXECUTIVE TO CHIEF JUSTICE

INTRODUCTION

William Howard Taft is the only American politician to have been both president of the United States and chief justice of the United States. That special distinction, while often noted, has not resulted in much sustained biographical attention to Taft's long public career. The standard two-volume biography of him, written by Henry F. Pringle and published in 1939, has withstood subsequent attempts to replace it.[1] Yet the Pringle book has many limitations, and obscures rather than illuminates its subject's historical significance. In 2011 Jonathan Lurie published the first of a two-volume biography covering Taft's life up to 1921, with a second projected volume to deal with the Supreme Court.[2] At 232 pages, however, Lurie's account does not delve in great depth into any specific phase of Taft's career during the period he covers.

Taft's presidency has attracted more attention. Two books in the 1970s examined his time in the White House. Donald F. Anderson used the president's personal papers and the perspective of a political scientist to provide "an in-depth study of one conservative's exercise of political power."[3] Paolo Coletta's *The Presidency of William Howard Taft* treated Taft as a political failure between the presidencies of Theodore Roosevelt and Woodrow Wilson.[4] In *William Howard Taft: An Intimate History*, Judith Icke Anderson focused on Taft's weight and his relationship with his wife Helen Herron Taft to explain his difficult years in the White House.[5]

I tried for a more analytic interpretation within the context of Republican and national politics in a book on Taft's presidency.[6]

Constitutional and legal scholars have devoted a great deal of time and energy to understanding Taft's tenure on the Supreme Court after 1921. Allen E. Ragan's *Chief Justice Taft* was an older survey of his leadership of the court.[7] A quarter of a century later Alpheus T. Mason provided what has become the standard work on Taft as chief justice.[8] Other books have looked at particular aspects of Taft and his court.[9]

As this review of the literature on Taft indicates, the eight years that he spent out of office and in private life have attracted little attention from his historians and biographers. Scholars note that he taught law and constitutional history at Yale University, opposed the nomination of Louis D. Brandeis to the Supreme Court in 1916, served on the National War Labor Board during World War I, was identified with the League to Enforce Peace and the fight for the League of Nations, and made up his differences with Theodore Roosevelt in 1917–1918. These cursory observations have exhausted historical interest in what might be called Taft's years in the political wilderness.

Finding Taft an intriguing and complex historical figure as president, I decided to explore what those eight years were like for the former chief executive. This book is the result of that endeavor. I discovered that from 1913 to 1921 Taft was involved in more causes and issues than previous writers had realized. There was an abundance of information about his work as president of the American Bar Association from 1913 to 1914. His service on the Commission to create the Lincoln Memorial revealed new information regarding that iconic part of monumental Washington. Taft was also immersed in the organization and service of the American Red Cross through his friend Mabel Boardman. In his relations with Woodrow Wilson and the Democratic administration, Taft became a persistent and sometimes strident critic of the government's policy toward the Philippine Islands.

These concerns meshed with the issues that have received more scrutiny about Taft. A major theme of this book is his interaction with Woodrow Wilson, in which Taft often supported the president in public while detesting him in private. Their ambivalent relationship had a significant impact on the battle over the League of Nations in 1919–1920. As a friend of the proposed league, Taft sought to promote American entry into an international organization while at the same time preserving his credentials within the Republican Party. The opposition of the Grand Old Party to anything identified with Wilson made Taft's task in this area complex and in the end frustrating.

Finally there was Theodore Roosevelt. For the first half of Taft's transitional eight years, he waged an intense effort within the Republican Party to marginalize his former friend and benefactor. Defeating Wilson was a goal they shared, but Taft did not want Roosevelt to regain a place of authority and power within the GOP just to oust Wilson from the White House. Once the United States entered World War I in April 1917, the common animus drew the one-time adversaries back into an awkward marriage of political convenience. By late 1918 it was "Will" and "Theodore" once again but that was largely a facade. Mistrust and doubt governed their collaboration.

Above all, Taft sought during this period to keep his options open to achieve his lifelong goal of becoming chief justice of the United States. The narrative illustrates how that ambition shaped his actions on all of these issues. While Taft's expediency and opportunism do not show him in the most positive light, he did accomplish what his heart had so long desired. In July 1921, his ambition was achieved and he reached his long-sought goal. A man often derided for his lack of political acumen made his way through the hazards of Republican affairs with some adroitness to gain his objective.

This account of Taft's journey from the White House to the Supreme Court thus fills a large gap in the life of an important American politician and jurist. It also discloses how intricate and complicated public affairs had become during the era of World War I and its aftermath. The clichés about Taft's weight, his maladroitness in the White House, and his conservatism of thought and doctrine have an element of truth, but they fail to do justice to a shrewd commentator on the political scene, a man of consummate ambition, and a resourceful practitioner of the internal politics of his party. I hope this study of Taft out of office will contribute to a better understanding of the society through which he moved to gain the ultimate prize he had so long coveted.

1

THE REJECTED PRESIDENT

On 4 March 1913, Will and Helen Taft slipped out of Washington, D.C., as the bands played and the crowds cheered for the inauguration of Woodrow Wilson as the twenty-eighth president. Four years earlier the Tafts had ridden together on a cold, snow-covered day from the Capitol to the White House to begin a presidency. Now, after a crushing defeat at the hands of Wilson and third-party candidate Theodore Roosevelt in November 1912, former president Taft was leaving for a vacation in the warm and friendly climes of Augusta, Georgia.

They went into a post-presidency that had none of the trappings that modern chief executives take with them upon leaving office. Taft simply became a private citizen again. There were no Secret Service agents to protect him, no pension to support his lifestyle, no government office where he might carry on whatever work he chose to pursue. All the splendor of the highest office in the land vanished at noon on 4 March 1913, and he now had to fend for himself in an uncertain political future. He had prestige, talent as a lawyer, and the goodwill of the American people, but that was all.

Taft believed that his political life was over. The Republicans would never nominate him for the presidency again. His most passionate desire to be chief justice of the United States also seemed remote, if not impossible. Woodrow Wilson would be president for four years, and had a good chance to serve eight. Taft would be sixty-three by 1921 and approaching the age when he would be too old to be named to the high court.

At the age of fifty-five, Taft needed a new career. Practicing law seemed a likely alternative, but questions at once arose in his mind. He had appointed so many judges to the federal bench, including five to the Supreme Court, that conflict of interest issues would occur when he appeared in courtrooms at all levels. He and Helen had saved money during their four years in the presidency, but the resulting income was far from enough to live on. What could he do that was both appropriate for a former president and profitable enough to sustain his lifestyle?

At the end of 1912, a suitable answer emerged. He received an invitation to teach at Yale University, his alma mater, as the Kent Professor of Law in Yale College. The position seemed ideal. With its flexible hours and light teaching duties, the professorship would enable him to make money as a public lecturer without seeming to be a professional orator or political operative. "I am coming back to Yale," he told the student newspaper in a letter of late February 1913. He intended to help young men "appreciate the Constitution of the United States, under which we have enjoyed so many blessings and under which we must work out our political and economic salvation."[1]

Before he took up his duties at Yale, Taft spent a month in Georgia recuperating from the rigors of his presidency and the sting of his defeat. When the couple reached Augusta on March 5, a large crowd of flag-waving school children, local military school cadets, and adult well-wishers greeted them at the train station. The now former president shook hands with many of the children and told the throng "that he was glad to get back to Augusta and more." He said to reporters that he expected to have "a quiet stay" and declined "to talk politics." On that note, eight years of Taft's post-presidency commenced.[2]

Until his crushing defeat at the hands of Wilson and Roosevelt, William Howard Taft's public career had been a string of political and personal successes. He had first been a local judge in his native Cincinnati, where he had been born in 1857. After attending Yale

Taft Leaves Office. William Howard Taft and the new president, Woodrow Wilson, posed for photographers on Inauguration Day, 4 March 1913. Taft was ready to lay down the burdens of office. (Library of Congress)

College and graduating in 1878, he had earned a law degree at the Cincinnati Law School and then become active in local politics. He served a brief term as collector of internal revenue and received an appointment as a judge of the Ohio Superior Court from Governor Joseph B. Foraker. He won his only election before the presidency in 1888 as an incumbent on the bench. "Like every well-connected Ohio man," Taft said of this phase of his life, "I always had my plate right side up when offices were falling."[3]

The offices came to him not just as an Ohio man, but soon as a rising national figure. President Benjamin Harrison nominated him as solicitor general in early 1890, and he made a good showing in the cases he argued before the United States Supreme Court. During these years, Taft and his wife Helen Herron Taft, whom he had married in 1886, became friendly with another ambitious Republican, Theodore Roosevelt. In 1892, the president named Taft to the Federal Court of Appeals for the Sixth District, a post he occupied for the next eight years. He often ruled against labor unions in the turbulence of the 1890s, but he did not worry about any electoral impact of his decisions. His hope was that the administration of William McKinley might in the near future elevate him to the United States Supreme Court.

A call came from the McKinley White House in early 1900 but not for a seat on the high court. Instead, the president asked Taft to serve on the Philippine Commission that he had charged with framing a civil government for the islands acquired from Spain after the war of 1898. Helen "Nellie" Taft wanted her husband to take the new post as a possible stepping-stone to the White House. She had visited the presidential mansion during the administration of Rutherford B. Hayes and hoped to return one day as first lady. Will Taft saw it as his duty to carry out the president's assignment, with the understanding that McKinley would take care of him as far as the Supreme Court was concerned.

Taft's four-year tenure in the Philippines made him a national political figure. His skill as an administrator and his rapport with the people of the archipelago helped make civil government a success, first for McKinley and soon for Theodore Roosevelt. In 1904,

Roosevelt invited him to return home and become secretary of war, succeeding Elihu Root. Taft and Roosevelt forged a close working partnership that in time led the president to see his friend as the logical Republican nominee in 1908. Had the position of chief justice of the United States become vacant during those years, Taft would have preferred that to a race for the presidency. No such vacancy occurred, and Taft declined two of Roosevelt's offers to go on the Court as an associate justice. Helen Taft, suspicious of Roosevelt's motives, urged her husband to remain eligible for the White House. She had ambitions to make Washington the social center of the nation, a goal that only a first lady could pursue.

By the time the 1908 race for the Republican nomination began, Taft had emerged as President Roosevelt's designated choice. With the backing of the administration and his own popularity within the party, Taft gained a first-ballot selection when the national convention met in Chicago in June 1908. He proved a more skilled campaigner than Republican professionals had anticipated. Roosevelt's public endorsement also helped Taft achieve a decisive success over the Democratic nominee, William Jennings Bryan, in November 1908.

From that moment of triumph, Taft's political fortunes, once so powerfully in his favor, experienced a downward turn. His friendship with Roosevelt frayed even before Taft's inauguration on 4 March 1909. In the presidency, Taft encountered a variety of setbacks and difficulties, as his judicial temperament made him a mundane contrast to the charisma and excitement of Roosevelt. Political troubles with the Payne-Aldrich Tariff of 1909 and the Ballinger-Pinchot controversy over conservation in 1909–1910 established the perception of ineptitude that Taft never overcame. Roosevelt had gone to Africa right after leaving the White House. Upon his return in June 1910, the awkwardness between the two men degenerated first into dislike, and then into outright opposition on Roosevelt's part in 1912.

The bitter campaign that Taft and Roosevelt waged for the Republican nomination in 1912 produced a lasting rupture. In the end, Taft's superior mastery of the delegate selection process carried him to a renomination. An angry Roosevelt, convinced that the nomination had been stolen, bolted and formed a third party. Meanwhile, the Democrats nominated Woodrow Wilson. With the Republicans split between the regulars who stood with Taft and the dissidents who joined Roosevelt's Progressive Party, Wilson cruised to an overwhelming electoral college blowout.

Taft carried only two states and ran a poor third to Roosevelt. Few presidents have been more rejected than William Howard Taft was in November 1912. The outgoing president took his defeat in good part, but the repudiation of his career left permanent scars, no matter how gracefully he denied the sting of the people's verdict.

The Tafts spent a month in Georgia in a relaxed mode that Will Taft had not enjoyed since he entered public service during the mid-1880s. It was, he told his doctor, "twenty-five days of almost unalloyed sweetness." By early April constant rounds of golf, the warm weather, and the absence of official cares had left Taft, in the words of one reporter, with "his cheeks ruddy with health and tanned by exposure to the Southern sun, eyes sparkling, and the same old cheery smile."[4] He told his doctor that "I am glad to say that Mrs. Taft seems to have profited by her stay at Augusta as much as I did."[5]

Both Tafts needed the rest they achieved. Four years in the presidency and general neglect of his health during decades of government service had left Taft in weakened condition. Even by the generous standards of his overall heft, he had gotten very fat as president. He now weighed in the neighborhood of 350 pounds, and his blood pressure had soared to dangerous levels. For many years he had disregarded the state of his teeth. While he was not yet in a serious physical crisis, Taft had good reason to be concerned about the medical trends he was experiencing.

The presidency years had also left Helen Taft in impaired health. She experienced two strokes during the White House years. The first and more serious event left her with impaired speech in May 1909. Another stroke in the spring of 1911 slowed her recuperation. Although she had played a constructive part in bringing classical music artists to Washington over the preceding four years, the exertions of being first lady had slowed her recovery from her illness. She now needed an extended rest and a chance to regain her physical stamina.[6]

On 1 April 1913 a large crowd greeted Helen and Will Taft at the New Haven train station. Two thousand undergraduates serenaded the couple as they made their way to the campus. In remarks at Willacy Hall, Taft said, "I cherish the opportunity of bringing all the little help I can to the young men now going out in life to become the leaders of thought in the Nation." He hoped to contribute "to the influence and expansion of the Yale spirit."[7]

While they looked for a house to rent in New Haven, the former president set up an office and residence on the sixth floor of the nearby Hotel Taft. Named for his brother Horace, the Hotel Taft had just opened in 1911, and provided ample office space for the former president on one floor. His working staff consisted of a single secretary, Wendell Mischler, who had been with Taft since his days in the War Department. Forty-two years old and a native of Ohio, Mischler handled Taft's correspondence, booked his lectures around the country, and managed his professional finances. Taft attested to his dependence on Mischler's hard work when he inscribed a photograph of himself to "my dear friend and indispensable co-worker, a model in accuracy, patience, foresight and loyalty, and without whose aid I could not do half the work I do."[8]

As a kind of advance agent in residence for the former president, Mischler pushed hard for the maximum returns for his boss. In the spring of 1913, Mischler told Taft about a proposed payment for reprinting some of his lectures in the *North American Review.* "I do not like the honorarium which he offers you—$1000 for eight lectures." Not everyone agreed with Mischler "as to the lucubrations of an ex-President," Taft told his brother Charles, "but still it is great insurance to have at hand an associate who is not restrained by modesty from claiming enough for his principal."[9]

Over the course of his vacation and the initial months in New Haven, Taft addressed his weight for the first time in more than a decade: he had last consulted a doctor prior to his presidential bid.[10] He commenced an informal diet that cut back on the huge portions he had been devouring. Fruits and vegetables assumed a larger place in his luncheon menu. As the days passed, the excess poundage receded toward the three-hundred-pound mark. By mid-May he had shed almost thirty pounds. The loss showed up in looser fitting clothes, and he had to rework his wardrobe. Nellie now anticipated "considerable cost in the altering of my clothes, and while on pleasure and beauty she is bent, she has a frugal mind."[11]

By the time Taft arrived in New Haven, it was too late in the academic year for him to offer a class. Instead, he prepared eight public lectures on the theme "Questions of Modern Government" that he delivered twice a week during May 1913. The press followed these talks with brief summaries of their content. The former president inveighed against what he regarded as the excesses of progressive reform and the nostrums Theodore Roosevelt had advanced during the preceding year. In his third lecture on 9 May, he likened the progressive proposals of the initiative and referendum to "legislation during the French Revolution—the work of political cranks and directly contrary to the spirit of the Constitution." In the next talk he denounced the recall as "a hair trigger to the bottom of politics."[12]

In the reading he did to prepare his lectures, Taft encountered the work of Charles A. Beard and his book *An Economic Interpretation of the Constitution of the United States* (1913). Beard's findings about the economic interests of the framers of the Constitution irritated the president. "Could lunacy go further?" a vexed Taft wrote to Elihu Root. "I suppose he [Beard] thinks it would have been better if he could have demonstrated that the members of the Constitutional Convention were not men of substance but were dead bodies, out-of-the-elbows demagogues, and cranks who never had any money and representatives of the purlieus of the population."[13]

Throughout the first phase of his post-presidency, Taft avoided any public comments on the performance of his successor. Woodrow Wilson had begun with dramatic events in his first weeks. His in-person address to Congress about what would become the Underwood Tariff broke more than a century of precedent. Then the

Democratic Congress tackled revision of the tariff, a process that Taft had found so difficult in 1909. Watching these events from New Haven, Taft decided not to offer any newspaper reactions to what the White House was doing. "If they are getting off on the right foot and will be successful, all right; if not, let them stew in their own juice." He told his close friend Mabel Boardman, the leader of the Red Cross, that "I have gotten fully used to reading the papers without my name in them, and it is not an unpleasant change."[14]

Taft had often procrastinated during his White House years in ways that left him scrambling to write speeches and prepare state papers at the last minute. In his new situation, free from the rigors of office, he worked on a more sustained and productive basis. Lectures, articles, and speeches on legal matters now engaged his revived energies, and he accomplished a prodigious amount of writing before he left for his regular vacation at Murray Bay, Canada, toward the end of June. He had missed the relaxation he found in the Canadian climate when he observed the existing custom and did not leave the boundaries of the United States as a sitting president.

Though he talked of a low profile, Taft took on a number of policy commitments and at least one long-running challenge to President Wilson's policies in this first year. Republicans in New Haven had been working for some time to secure a new post office building. They had obtained a $450,000 appropriation for the structure before Taft left office. In the autumn of 1913, a question arose over what kind of material, granite or marble, would be used in the construction of the building. Taft's lobbying with the Wilson administration persuaded Secretary of the Treasury William G. McAdoo to use the Tennessee marble that Taft wanted rather than the less expensive granite originally proposed.[15] A similar issue on a more national scale involved the building of the memorial to Abraham Lincoln in Washington, D.C., that had been authorized during the Taft administration. Congress had created a commission, with Taft as its chair, to supervise the planning and then the construction of a suitable memorial to the martyred president. By the time Taft left office, he and his colleagues had selected architect Henry Bacon to design the structure and had chosen the site in Washington where the memorial would rise. Democrats in Congress looked with some skepticism at Republican efforts to memorialize the greatest hero of the Grand Old Party. There was even a resolution in Congress, sponsored by William Borland, a Missouri Democrat, to replace Taft and the other Republicans on the bipartisan commission with Democrats. When the press asked Taft about that proposal, he responded: "I suppose I might stand the loss. It wasn't much when they took the Presidency away, but I tell you if they do likewise with this job it will hurt."[16]

The next phase of the process of constructing the memorial, like the New Haven post office, was to select the material that would comprise the structure itself. While the commission would make a recommendation, the ultimate decision rested with Lindley M. Garrison, the new secretary of war, who had the authority to sign contracts and supervise the construction. Henry Bacon wanted to use a marble that came from the west, Colorado-Yule white marble, quarried by the George A. Fuller Company. Other bidders from the South challenged the value of the Colorado-Yule product and raised doubts about the fairness of the process by which the Fuller firm had been selected. Impressed with the protests from Democratic lawmakers on behalf of Georgia marble, Secretary Garrison asserted his authority over the selection process that had produced the Colorado-Yule decision. The delays that Garrison's actions introduced into the work of the commission irritated Taft. He called the secretary "an agreeable man, full of professions of liberality and independence," but someone who was "not a heavy weight, judging by his construction of the statute."[17]

The controversy over the marble continued into early 1914 before Garrison yielded and accepted the verdict of the commission about the Colorado-Yule marble. Work on the memorial then proceeded during the rest of Wilson's first term. Taft resented what he regarded as an unnecessary delay in moving the Lincoln Memorial forward. The episode aroused suspicions in his mind about Garrison as an administrator, and these spilled over into a more substantive policy area, the attitude of the White House and the

Democrats toward continued American rule in the Philippine Islands. As a result, in 1913 Taft began a personal campaign to frustrate Democratic attempts to frame eventual independence for the archipelago.

The Democratic platform in 1912 denounced the acquisition of the Philippines as an "inexcusable blunder which has involved us in enormous expense." Instead, the party advocated "an immediate declaration of the nation's purpose to recognize the independence of the Philippine Islands as soon as a stable government can be established" with the United States to guarantee independence and retain "coaling stations and naval bases." Taft and the Republicans noted the hedged nature of the Democratic pledge and the vague timetable for eventual independence.[18]

What the Democrats were proposing to the Philippines seemed to Taft misleading and unworkable. While he regarded the Filipino people with affection and a certain degree of respect, he did not believe that they would be capable of self-government for many years. His sense of when they might be prepared to take control of their own destiny was so vague that it lacked any specific content. The Filipino people, he wrote in October 1913, were a "great mass of ignorance" and thus he concluded that no "foundations for self-government, let alone independence, are yet present in the Philippines."[19]

The Wilson administration did not, however, share Taft's view of the Philippine situation. The president decided to appoint a governor general for the islands who would accelerate the process of turning affairs over to native politicians. In so doing, they selected a man whose appointment outraged Taft and the supporters of his views about the Philippines. Francis Burton Harrison had served five terms in the House of Representatives, from New York. In 1910 he had criticized then-President Taft over his handling of the Ballinger-Pinchot controversy. Taft had refused to see Harrison when he came to the White House. Added to the personal bad blood between the two men was Taft's perception that Harrison had remarried in haste after the death of his wealthy wife in 1905. In private letters, Taft called Harrison "an opportunist" who was "political to the ends of his fingers." If Taft had needed any further reason to oppose Wilson on the Philippines, the Harrison selection provided ample motivation.[20]

While claiming that he was not in partisan politics, Taft soon found opportunities to assail the Philippine policy of the new administration. On 10 June he addressed the Philippine Society in New York as did the Philippine delegate to Congress, Manuel Quezon. Both men quoted President Wilson to suit their own arguments, but Taft maintained that if granted independence "the freedom and liberty would not be preserved for all the people" of the islands "as we are preserving it now."[21]

Taft believed that the Wilson administration was deceiving itself and the people of the Philippines. In private, Democratic officials told him that they did not intend to provide independence in the way that the Filipinos expected but, in the words of Secretary of War Garrison, "they must do something." When Francis Harrison arrived in the islands, he told his audiences, "Every step we take will be taken with a view to the ultimate independence of the Islands and as a preparation for that independence." To Taft, Harrison's assertions were "improvident steps" designed to mislead the Filipinos about the ultimate purpose of the government in Washington. In an article and then in a speech in Brooklyn in November 1913, he reiterated his case for staying in the Philippines and avoiding making promises of independence that could not be fulfilled.[22]

Taft may have thought that his criticism of the new administration and its Philippine policy was meant in a constructive spirit. Yet he seemed to go out of his way to needle the occupant of the White House. In December 1913 the Military Order of the Carabao, a group of army officers serving and retired who had been in the Philippines, held its annual banquet. Featured were satirical attacks on the policy of the White House toward the islands. An offended president was reported to be "much incensed at the conduct of old and prominent officers in ridiculing the Administration's policies" and he asked the secretaries of the War Department and the Navy Department for an investigation.[23]

Taft waded into the controversy at a dinner in honor of William

Francis Burton Harrison. Taft was a bitter enemy of Harrison's administration as governor general of the Philippines during the Wilson presidency. (Library of Congress CL-DIG-ggbain-14384)

Cameron Forbes, a former governor general of the Philippines under the Republicans. In his remarks, Taft indicated that the White House had overreacted in its anger at the Carabao diners. The dinner guests from the army were only reflecting previous feelings, and their songs "are not to be construed in the present attitude of the army toward the Filipino." In fact it was the administration, he contended, that was "only reviving the feeling that existed when the army was there."[24]

Taft's public opposition irritated President Wilson. He lumped the former president in with another critic of his Philippine approach, Dean C. Worcester. Wilson did not believe that these naysayers would "be able to do much damage, but it is the more important in view of what they are doing that we should handle the facts with a sense of reality and know what we are about." There the matter rested after Wilson's opening year in office. Taft would return to the attack in the months that followed.[25]

Of all the activities to which he committed himself in the first year of political retirement, Taft was most devoted to the improvement of the state of the legal profession. He was intent on preserving the role of the judiciary against the recall, and to fight against what he regarded as the dangerous proposals of Theodore Roosevelt and the Progressives. In that campaign, he focused his energies on the future of the American Bar Association (ABA). The lawyers were meeting outside of the United States in Montreal, Canada, in a precedent-setting departure from their normal sessions in the United States. Taft was on the official program to give a speech on "The Selection and Tenure of Judges." He was also committed to speak to the assembled attorneys on "the influence of legal education on sociological progress."[26]

For his speech on the latter topic, Taft corresponded with such legal scholars as Roscoe Pound of Harvard and Henry M. Bates of the University of Michigan about the desirability of requiring graduation from a law school as a prerequisite for admission to the bar examination. Pound contended that the profession required "a properly educated and properly trained bar," which would have "bar examiners be brought into better relations with our best law schools and that modern and scientific instruction in the law rather than the so-called practical instruction of the purely money-making school be furthered and not repressed by the machinery of admission to the bar."[27]

Taft had doubts regarding some of Pound's innovative ideas about the way lawyers should be trained. "I don't know quite how sound he is," he told his nephew Will Herron, who worked in the Department of Justice, "and I cannot but feel that he is somewhat disposed, as he himself criticizes in some judges, to pedantry. However, he is so fruitful of suggestion and so full of learning that one gets much value from him." In the area of legal education, the ideas of Pound and Taft overlapped. The former president was eager to preach to his colleagues the virtues of greater professionalism at the bar.[28]

The ABA meeting in Montreal proved a triumph for Taft. One annual ritual was the selection of a president for the association to serve a one-year term. A prominent Georgia attorney named Peter Meldrim had been planning for some years to gain the prestige of the post. A former mayor of Savannah, he was "a standing candidate for the Presidency because he has attended the meeting every year. He was trying to set up his election by calling upon those he had pledged to vote for him in years gone by."[29]

A number of Taft's friends put his name in nomination and the lawyers in the group's executive council then voted. The first result was a tie with Meldrim. A second ballot produced a small majority for Taft and his nomination was then made unanimous. "I hope," Taft wrote his half-brother, "that we may break up the system of pledging and buttonholing and political wirepulling, because under such a system mediocre men come to the front, and the Association is not helped." In Taft's mind, his victory reflected a spirit of reform within the ABA. It was not clear that he was able to do much to change the way the group worked to choose its leader in his one-year term. Two years later, however, Peter Meldrim won the prize.[30]

In one key area a former member of Taft's cabinet, Jacob M. Dickinson, sought to maintain an all-white membership of the association. A year earlier, three black lawyers were elected to the association in part by accident. Dickinson then offered a resolution to direct local councils of the association to inform the larger body whenever an African American lawyer was proposed for membership. The rationale was "it has never been contemplated that members of the colored race should become members of this Association." Dickinson's resolution was adopted. As the 1913 meeting loomed, however, Dickinson feared that civil rights activist Morefield Storey was again going to raise the issue.[31]

Because the meeting was outside of the United States, Storey agreed not to bring up the racial question at Montreal. Instead, he accepted a proposal from a southern member to have the issue submitted to the next annual meeting. There would be briefs prepared by Storey and his opponents, and then a vote at the next gathering without any substantive discussion. However, since there was some sentiment to meet outside of the United States again in 1914, it remained unclear whether the racial composition of the ABA would be aired at all. In fact it would be decades before the group admitted black members.[32]

In addition to Taft's election as president of the ABA, his speeches received a very positive reception. His advocacy of improved legal education attracted strong newspaper attention. All in all, he reported to his brother, "it was really a very delightful occasion." The presence of the British jurist and politician, Lord Haldane, made for a glittering assembly of attorneys from Canada, Great Britain, and the United States. At a time when the legal profession was in disrepute in the United States, American attorneys gained from association with the Canadian bar. In his address to the final banquet, Taft observed to his Canadian hosts that "the reason why we are having such a good time here is because coming over from the United States with a somewhat shady reputation for the whole profession we have been rehabilitated by your welcome."[33]

Upon his return from Canada, Taft began an activist term as the public leader of the American legal profession. One of his most important duties was to select lawyers for the various policy committees of the association. For Taft that meant favoring those attorneys who agreed with his ideological attitudes. The ABA's committee on legislative drafting included Louis D. Brandeis as one of its members. Brandeis also sat on the panel dealing "with uniform judicial procedure." Remembering his intense battle with the Boston lawyer during the Ballinger-Pinchot controversy of 1909–1910, Taft believed that Brandeis had no place in the deliberations of key bar association panels. He removed Brandeis from both slots.[34]

Proponents of progressive measures that Taft disliked also had to give way. "I don't want to be associated in the question of jurisprudence with any man that favors a recall of judicial decisions, and I find the name of William Draper Lewis on your list. I think it ought to be stricken out." Although he was the dean of the law school at the University of Pennsylvania, Lewis had also committed the political sin of identifying with Theodore Roosevelt and serving on the resolutions committee of the Progressive Party in 1912.[35]

Taft's term coincided with a major historical milestone that led to a provocative idea about where the bar association should meet in 1914. The centennial of the Treaty of Ghent, which ended the War of 1812 and launched the century of Anglo-American peace, prompted some ABA members to propose the idea of having the organization gather in London in the mid-summer of 1914. The leading proponent of a British session was James M. Beck, a conservative Republican, "who has had a good many London associations with English lawyers." There was enough interest in the idea at first that Taft wrote to Lord Haldane. "In invading another country as we would do, we would like to know that our brothers of the profession would wish to have us."[36]

While Taft waited for the English response to his proposal, opposition to the idea of another meeting outside of the United States was gathering within the ABA. It had been an innovation to assemble in Montreal, and there had been some grumbling about that session even with all of its ceremonial success. The dean of the Harvard Law School noted that if the London meeting occurred it would mean that "our British associations would seem to be growing on us apace."[37]

Significant logistical problems soon emerged. Booking steamship passage for a major contingent of attorneys raised difficult questions of cost and timing. For average members of the bar, a trip to England from the southern or western United States would involve a significant expense and, more importantly, a large amount of time away from their legal practice. Others, such as the prominent Chicago attorney and longtime Taft friend, Max Pam, warned that "it would be said by some that there is a pandering to foreign attention and English glitter."[38]

Negative opinions from such figures as Joseph Hodges Choate, a former ambassador in London and venerable legal figure, combined with a certain degree of coolness from Lord Haldane, made it clear that a trip to England would not work in 1914. Taft concluded that having a regular meeting in the United States represented the consensus of the association's members. With that he turned his energies to finding a suitable city for the annual meeting.[39]

Though some lawyers advocated a meeting in Cincinnati, Taft spoke out for Washington as the site in autumn of 1914. He sought to give the gathering a "Pan-American color" with "no people from across the water." The chief justice of Canada would appear along with the Argentinian minister to the United States, Romulo S. Naon. Taft told Chief Justice Edward Douglass White that "I think I can count, from what I know, on strong expressions in all the addresses in favor of conservatism and constitutional government and the proper place of the courts."[40]

Being president of the ABA and his work on the Lincoln Memorial Commission did not exhaust Taft's activities devoted to the national capital. Through his friendship with Mabel Boardman, the guiding spirit of the American Red Cross, the former president also took a close interest in the affairs of that charitable organization. He and Mabel Boardman had known each other for many years and had established an affectionate, platonic working relationship. They were "Mabel" and "Will" in their letters, and Boardman's sympathetic ear meant much to Will Taft. "During my life in Washington," he wrote her in February 1913, "you have done so much to add to my happiness and my comfort and that of those dear to me that I feel as if I could not convey to you how much I appreciate it."[41]

Though she held no official leadership position in the Red Cross, Boardman had emerged as the directing presence of the group since she and her allies had ousted the founder, Clara Barton, in 1904. Boardman had alleged that Barton had been misusing the funds of the Red Cross for her own personal benefit, among other reasons for her departure. The episode left very hard feelings among Barton's supporters in Washington and around the country. However, both Theodore Roosevelt and Will Taft gave Boardman and her allies strong support. In the decade that followed, Boardman sought to introduce bureaucratic procedures into the functioning of the Red Cross to make it more efficient and more accountable.[42]

By 1913, Boardman had accomplished much of that agenda, but the organization was still under-funded and dependent on the largesse of the federal government. The Red Cross had no permanent headquarters in the capital. It relied on offices loaned to it from the War Department or rented around Washington, had a small membership, and still needed a cadre of volunteers to carry out its mission. In these conditions, Mabel Boardman wrote, "it is very difficult to do justice to the important work of the society."[43]

Sectional politics shaped how Congress responded to the appeals of the Red Cross. Southern lawmakers saw the organization as oriented toward the northern heritage of the Civil War. So Boardman and her allies had to work through a proposal for a structure that would honor "the women of the civil war." Congress appropriated some $400,000 for the edifice, and the Red Cross undertook to raise another $300,000 toward the total cost of $700,000. Taft congratulated Boardman on "the tremendous victory for the Red Cross that you have won" when Congress acted. He was prepared to help his friend raise the rest of the needed funds.[44]

Taft approached the wealthy philanthropist Mrs. Russell Sage, who had herself worked in a hospital as a volunteer during the Civil War before marrying her rich husband once the war was over. "There are few women of the Civil War now surviving who are in a position to contribute substantially," Taft wrote Sage, who was in her eighties at the time of his letter. "There would be special appropriateness in having such a monument erected by a woman, and by a woman who had her part in these stirring times." She contributed $50,000 and, with other donations, the Red Cross announced in December 1913 that the new building would become a reality.[45]

Throughout his first year of political retirement, Taft told friends that he was out of the partisan arena and, within understandable limits of his Republican allegiance, hoped for the success of Woodrow Wilson as president. Though he was sincere in these assertions, Will Taft told intimates about his persistent distrust of his successor's emerging record. He was also somewhat naive or disingenuous to believe that he could oppose the administration's policy in the Philippines and not be seen in the White House as a foe of the administration.

On the surface, he and Wilson were cordial to each other in public and friendly in private. Taft and Mabel Boardman went to the White House on 7 June 1913 to lunch with Wilson and members of his family. One of the guests reported that "it was such fun to hear the President and the Ex-President swap stories. I just *love* Mr. Taft; he is the most genial, kindly gentleman; and his geniality hasn't any of the rough undignified quality that that of so many men has." Taft told the Wilson circle that he was "very happy and *care-free*" and "sometimes he feels he ought to knock on wood for fear the old nightmare will come back—of being President! He didn't use the word nightmare but something like it."[46]

In his private correspondence, however, Taft let loose about his skeptical opinions regarding Wilson's performance in the White House. He concluded that the new president was a cynical opportunist who adopted positions based on questions of expediency rather than intrinsic merit (as Taft always believed he had done in the presidency). For information about what Wilson was doing, Taft relied on his reading of the newspapers and the gossip and inside information that his friends and contacts supplied him. A major source of insights were the frequent letters of Gus Karger, the Washington correspondent for the *Cincinnati Times-Star*, the newspaper that his half-brother Charles P. Taft owned. Karger approached the Wilson administration and the Democratic Congress from a partisan perspective, but his factual assertions seem to have

Gus J. Karger. The Washington reporter for the major Cincinnati newspaper, Karger kept Taft well informed on the Washington scene. (Library of Congress LC-DIG-npcc-02994)

been reliable about affairs in the capital. As Taft addressed public issues and required documentation, Karger said, "I'll be glad to help you dig up any material available here, if you should feel the need of it."[47]

Like other Republicans, Taft watched with a mixture of awe and envy as Woodrow Wilson and the Democrats put together a very successful first year in 1913. The majority party lowered tariff rates through the Underwood Tariff law and then late in 1913 passed the Federal Reserve Act to reform the nation's ineffective banking system. Such Wilsonian innovations as addressing Congress in person for the first time in more than a century attested to the presence of a new political force in national affairs. "I think Wilson has gotten off on the right foot," Taft told Elihu Root in early May. "He is bound to sink or swim according to the operation of his tariff."[48]

Though he knew that he had no hope of ever being a candidate in national politics again, Taft did want to see the Republican Party follow the conservative course he had outlined for it in 1912. To that end, he framed an article on the future of the Grand Old Party for *Cosmopolitan Magazine,* a publication owned by William Randolph Hearst. In the drafts that he circulated to Republican friends, he sought "to sustain the conservative element in the Republican party."[49] He contended that the Republicans had been affirmative in the past, but their major duty at that time was "the rescue of the country from the serious danger to which it is exposed in this attempted undermining of our stable civil liberties."[50] Taft completed the article only to find that Hearst and his associates wanted to place it in other parts of the publisher's empire. Disputes over that issue delayed the appearance of the essay for the rest of 1913.

By the end of 1913, Taft had become very disillusioned with his successor. He resented the change in Philippine policy, which he regarded as a repudiation of all that he had done in the islands. For Wilson's secretary of state William Jennings Bryan, he had nothing but contempt for his "utter ignorance" in the handling of foreign policy. Taft was skeptical of the long-term effects of the Underwood Tariff and he feared, in the case of the proposed Federal Reserve legislation, "we will injure business and for a poor banking system give use a worse one."[51]

Taft saved his most stinging private attacks for the way Wilson and Bryan had handled the revolution that swept Mexico after the ouster of Porfirio Díaz in 1911 and the murder of Francisco Madero in 1913 during the waning days of Taft's presidency. The Wilson White House had struggled to find a viable approach to the unrest south of the Rio Grande. They had rejected the government of Victoriano Huerta and sought his ouster from office and departure from Mexico itself. Making that happen proved elusive during 1913, and as 1914 began, the Wilson administration seemed confused about what it sought to accomplish.

"Could anything be more botched than this Mexican business,"

Taft asked Charles D. Hilles in September 1913. Taft concluded that "Bryan is achieving a greater sublimity as an ass than I thought it possible. They have made their trouble in Mexico and they might have avoided it." As he told his brother four weeks later, the president was "boiling over with indignation" about affairs in Mexico "that he is willing to risk everything to maintain that position, even a war of intervention."[52] Taft thus deemed Wilson to be failing in both the handling of Mexico and the Philippine problems. His conviction that the occupant of the White House was little more than a cynical opportunist intensified.

As the first full year of his post-presidency neared its end, William Howard Taft had reason to be content with the new position he had made for himself. The arrangement with Yale had provided him with just the right forum to launch political pronouncements without being seen as an overt partisan. His writing and lecturing supplied him with an income that sustained the lifestyle he and his wife preferred. Helen Taft, with the help of her daughter, had assembled her recollections in a book that would appear in 1914 about her years in the Philippines and the White House.[53]

In politics, the Republican Party had remained conservative, and Theodore Roosevelt's efforts to continue the Progressive Party were in obvious difficulty as 1914 approached. Taft told Walter L. Fisher, who had served in his cabinet as secretary of the interior, that he was "very, very busy, and yet the work does not tell on me near as much as less constant application in an office with such responsibility as that of the Presidency. No one can tell what a burden is lifted when he lays down the cares of an office like that."[54]

Like many Republicans, Taft anticipated that the 1914 congressional elections would see his party make gains in Congress and lay the basis for the defeat of Wilson in 1916. The eruption of World War I in Europe in the late summer of 1914 brought Taft into a new role as a former president. He intensified his earlier commitments to mechanisms that would restore peace once the fighting stopped. In so doing, he embarked on the campaign first for a League to Enforce Peace and then for a League of Nations that would define the rest of his postpresidential experience.

2

"WAR IS A DREADFUL THING"

For William Howard Taft, like most Americans, 1914 broke into two distinct sections. In the first seven months of the year, he followed the now-familiar pattern of teaching at Yale, traveling to give lectures, and writing about judicial and political issues. With the outbreak of World War I in August, Taft became involved with American efforts to prevent future wars through the League to Enforce Peace. That commitment would shape the course of his post-presidential career for the next seven years. It would both hinder and then facilitate his eventual appointment as chief justice of the United States in 1921.

As the new year opened, Will Taft had good reason to be contented with his life after the White House. His teaching at Yale had proved successful. He had a light schedule that left him sufficient time to pursue lecturing several times a week for lucrative fees. A reporter for the *Washington Herald* who visited his classes during late 1913 concluded that Taft "finds himself as popular as any instructor or professor at Yale." On Mondays and Tuesdays at 10:30 a.m., he joined his law school students in Hendrie Hall for an hour's talk on constitutional issues.[1]

As Kent Professor of Law in Yale College, Taft offered a course in constitutional law for undergraduates in Osborn Hall. "An elective for seniors, the class attracted a large audience at first and then diminished somewhat in its appeal. Taft started out to have students recite in each class, and the students exercised a good deal of cleverness in figuring out who might be called on during any given class. To involve more students in the work of the course, Professor Taft worked out, with student advice, a system of required daily papers that stimulated better attendance.[2]

When he stuck to his prepared text, Taft was a somewhat dry lecturer. What made his comments memorable occurred when something he said reminded him of an issue or problem he had confronted during his political career. After lowering his head and peering over his glasses, he would tell a story or anecdote that soon had "every man in the room . . . shaking with laughter." But his course was anything but a cinch. "If you don't study your lessons, you'll regret it at the time of the examination."[3]

Whenever he gave examinations, Taft did all the grading himself. He took the students' papers with him on his frequent trips and used them as an excuse to fend off intrusive individuals on train trips or in stations. Like many another faculty member, he found the grading task wearying. As he told Mabel Boardman in February 1914, "I have about 110 to correct, and they take me from seven to ten minutes apiece, so you can see what a bore they are." He added quickly, "I must not kick about it because that is the 'lien' of the Professor's life and I would not be satisfied to let anybody else do the work for me, as some of the Professors do."[4]

Taft was not impressed with the students he had encountered, and he resisted attempts at Yale to institute an honor system for the taking of examinations. He expected that cheating would occur if the professor were not present to supervise the testing process. In any event, "there are a great many who will take advantage" of the teacher's absence "to be disorderly and loud and conversational." He concluded that "the manners of the present generation of University students might be very much bettered." Out of these ruminations came an article for *Ladies' Home Journal* on "The College Slouch."[5]

On the one hand, Taft found that "the environment in our present universities is better adapted to the moral training and elevation of a young man than it was thirty or forty years ago." Yet he also noted "the lack of physical discipline" among the students,

Taft with Mabel Boardman. Taft and his close friend, Mabel Boardman, collaborated on the business of the American Red Cross until he eased her out of power after the outbreak of World War I. (Library of Congress LC-DIG-npcc-05070)

which came along with "the lack of erect bearing, the indifferent manners and slouchy dress among the students." These trends had long been present among undergraduates, Taft conceded, "but I think it is exaggerated in the present day, and that steps might be taken to restrain it." Taft particularly criticized students who chewed gum or smoked. Like many of his colleagues at Yale, he watched for evidence of dissipation and loose morals.[6]

In the case of the hotel where he lived and maintained his offices in New Haven, the former president became exercised, along with the Yale administration, at the presence of dancing and chorus girls in the Grill Room of the Hotel Taft. This mix enabled "the young men of the College to dissipate." Since the Taft was named after his brother Horace, he wanted to ensure that "it should not be regarded as a source of evil in the University." He wrote letters to the management of the hotel warning them of the possible dire consequences if the practice of late-night dancing were not ended.[7] In the end, the students who had been the major participants "have left College at the intimation of the Dean" while the chorus girls also departed for new roles elsewhere.[8]

By early 1914, Taft had worked out a weekly routine that enabled him to lecture across the eastern half of the United States while carrying out his teaching duties at Yale during the first half of each week. Wendell Mischler had mastered the train schedules so that he could book his principal as far west as Iowa and still get him back to New Haven in time for his classroom responsibilities. Taft had prepared a series of legal and current topics for all kinds of audiences.

Enjoying the whole process of traveling, the former president adapted to the rigors of the road much as he had done in the White House. "I guess I have been a pretty good traveler," he told an interviewer in 1921, "or else I would not have stood it all." He attributed his success to his ability to sleep anywhere: on trains, in cars, and in boats. Taft insisted on the most modern conveniences. "It is not hard to rest in the modern Pullman car when one is accustomed to travel. In comfort, with all the conveniences, I can travel anywhere, any time, without tiring." While the monetary rewards from his speeches were the ostensible reason for Taft's wanderings, Archie Butt had it right during the White House years. "The President takes these trips just as a dipsomaniac goes on periodical sprees." Butt concluded that "it is almost freakish, the ghoulish delight he gets from traveling."[9]

The highlight of his journeying during the early months of 1914 was the visit he paid to Canada in late January. In a lengthy letter to Mabel Boardman, he recounted the warm welcome that Canadian officials accorded him both in Toronto and Ottawa. In his formal addresses, he warned his Canadian audiences that they could face the same kind of corrupt influences in their politics that had troubled the United States. The personal highlights for Taft were his conversations with the Duke of Connaught and his wife. The Duchess said that she had admired Theodore Roosevelt and then concluded that "she had made a mistake in talking that way to me, considering my relations with Roosevelt." Taft responded that he had been "a very warm friend of Roosevelt and had greatly admired him and that it did not hurt me to talk to me on the subject of Roosevelt or any other subject that pleased her Royal Highness."[10]

During one of the final informal meetings, the wife of the lieutenant governor, Mrs. John Gibson, "challenged me to a dance in the beautiful ballroom." An aide played "The Blue Danube" on the piano and the couple swirled around the floor. "Mrs. Gibson is a beautiful dancer," Taft recalled, "so we got along very pleasantly, and I found that my wind since I have lost weight is a good deal better for dancing than it used to be." In the free and easy atmosphere, Taft felt "as if I were home for the holidays at a country home."[11]

While he was no longer an active politician, Taft did enjoy seeing the fortunes of the Republican Party improve during the first half of the year. His article about the GOP that he had originally written for *Cosmopolitan* had become enmeshed in the editorial practices of the magazine's owner, William Randolph Hearst, and in the end the article appeared in the *Saturday Evening Post*, which published it in mid-February under the title "The Future of the Republican Party."[12]

As the newspapers covered the appearance of Taft's article, they reported "Taft-Roosevelt Feud Still Bitter." "No man and no party in the country," read the text of Taft's piece, "have done so much to destroy the confidence of the people in the justice of the courts and in the existence of any possible independent judiciary as have Roosevelt and the Progressive Party." Since Roosevelt's "new theories of government will seriously impair that which we hold essential in the maintenance of liberty regulated by law," Taft argued that his party was justified "in thinking that the most important thing to the country is to defeat the Progressive party in presidential elections."[13]

Taft wanted his article to have influence, especially against any attempt to allow Roosevelt back into the Republican ranks. He was pleased with those who wrote him endorsing his sentiments. "It has aroused considerable bitterness on the part of some extreme Progressive Republicans who would like to see Roosevelt nominated as a Republican." On the whole, the essay accomplished what Taft wanted in the way of making his fellow party members resist any attempt to reach out to the Roosevelt camp. Meanwhile, he reaffirmed his conviction that he was out of politics. At an address to the Young Men's Republican Club in New Haven, he said: "I don't expect to hold office again. I'm up an apple tree looking at the show, but I have not given up my love for the party or my belief that in the party lies the hope of the country."[14]

With the exception of his strictures about the Philippines, Taft kept his private criticism of the Wilson administration out of the newspapers. Nonetheless, he enjoyed his success over the secretary of war, Lindley M. Garrison, in the long-running battle about the marble for the Lincoln Memorial that had taken place during 1913. Taft believed that Garrison had delayed approving the choice of the commission over the marble to be used in the memorial because of pressure from Georgia lawmakers in Washington who lobbied for their home state's product. He was angered when Garrison announced that he would hold a public hearing on the issue in mid-January 1914.

In the end, the question of the marble was laid before the government's Commission of Fine Arts, which ruled that the Colorado-Yule product was superior to the Georgia alternative. That action

Taft with Members of the Lincoln Memorial Commission, 1920. Taft served with Democratic leader Champ Clark (left), Joseph G. Cannon (beard), and Samuel W. McCall on the commission to create a memorial to Abraham Lincoln. (Library of Congress LC-DIG-npcc-01185)

gave the secretary of war an out to end the controversy and to sign the contracts that enabled the construction of the memorial to go forward. Taft believed that he had prevailed on the merits but was also pleased at the implied rebuke to Secretary Garrison. "I have a feeling of intense satisfaction in having beaten the Secretary of War in that Lincoln Memorial business." Garrison, he concluded, was "a very small potato."[15]

Garrison, however, was the man in charge of much of the Philippine policy of the Wilson presidency. By defeating him over the memorial, Taft had alienated an adversary who could respond to the criticisms that the former president made about what was happening in that "Asian" possession. The rivalry between the two men would flare again in 1915 as Taft continued to assail the administration's handling of the archipelago and its potential independence from American hegemony.

Arbitration of disputes between nations had been one of the major elements of Taft's foreign policy in the White House. He never ceased to regret that Theodore Roosevelt and Republicans in the Senate had blocked the pacts he and the State Department had negotiated to install arbitration procedures in 1911–1912. He pursued world peace as a personal goal and offered optimistic assessments of European leaders in furtherance of that objective. In June 1913, for example, he told the *New York Times* that Kaiser Wilhelm II of Germany had "been, for the last quarter of a century, the greatest single force in the practical maintenance of peace in the world." As for the prospect of "universal peace" among nations, he was more cautious in October 1913. "In spite of the Balkans and Mexico and China, settlements of difficulties by agreement and arbitration increases. Prophecy as to rapidity of its progress is futile."[16]

During the spring of 1914, Taft laid out his views on arbitration, international law, and the potential for the world community to take effective action for peace in an elaborate series of articles for the influential journal, the *Independent*. The essays became the former president's most sustained statement of his position on these issues before the outbreak of World War I. They also anticipated much of what Taft would say in the campaign for the League to Enforce Peace once the hostilities had commenced. Little noticed by his major biographer, Henry F. Pringle, and other students of Taft's life, the essays offer an interesting insight into his legal thinking on international law. The genesis of the series was an invitation from the New York Peace Society in September 1913 to give four lectures on various aspects of American foreign policy and the quest for international peace. The lectures would be under the copyright of the *Independent* and its publisher, the peace activist, Hamilton Holt. There was talk of book publication. In the end, however, the series appeared in the *Independent* during the spring of 1914.[17]

The series opened with an article in February 1914 that called for greater power for the federal government to find and punish

Americans who violated the civil rights of aliens through mob law or lynching. Taft argued that "the whole prosecuting and detective machinery" of the federal government should be deployed to bring to trial perpetrators who allegedly lynched aliens. To that purpose he wanted "valid Federal legislation" giving presidents and courts the jurisdiction they needed to bring such abuses of treaty obligations to an end.[18]

In subsequent articles, Taft defended the principles he had followed when he negotiated arbitration treaties with Great Britain and France during his presidency. His critics at the time, most notably Theodore Roosevelt, had claimed that the pacts had too broad a definition of what were "justiciable" subjects. Moreover, the United States might find itself on the losing side if some of the cases were to go before an international court. The Senate had watered down the treaties and Taft had withdrawn them. Still, he went on, "I was anxious to give a model to the world of a treaty that meant something in the matter of arbitration."[19]

Out of office and free to speak and write his true thoughts, Taft defended the choices he had made. He wanted a broad definition of justiciable subjects, and he did not see it as a political calamity that the United States might lose a case, especially when the facts ran against the American side. He even went so far as to advocate a solution for enforcing court decisions that limited American sovereignty. To carry out such a ruling, "it may, at first require an international police force to carry out the judgments, but the public opinion of nations would accomplish much, and with such a system we could count on a gradual reduction of armaments and a feeling of the same kind of security that the United States and Canada have today which makes armaments and navies on our northern border entirely unnecessary."[20]

In two more essays for the *Independent* during the spring of 1914, Taft laid out the historical precedents for international federations of nations to resolve disputes, and then discussed how such a scheme might work in the world of 1914. The argument became a little more vague at this point. Taft alluded to the increasing communication among nations and other conditions that, in his mind, made for progress. "The united spirit of search for truth and the promotion of world brotherhood shown in the universities the world over, and the gradual forming of a world public opinion" created an environment in which the trend toward greater judicial settlement of international disputes would be able to thrive. As for enforcement of a court's decrees, again public opinion would rule. Taft then passed the buck to the future. "When a judgment of the court is defied, it will be time enough to prevent the recurrence of such an international breach of faith."[21]

Events in Europe would soon overtake Taft's faith in judicial resolution of international disputes and render his optimism about world opinion moot until peace returned to the world. In its elements, however, Taft's proposal would spill over into his forthcoming commitment to the League to Enforce Peace after the end of World War I. He would never lose a lawyer's conviction that an international courtroom was the proper forum for resolving the problems that divided nations and produced wars.

After a year out of the presidency, Taft gave every appearance of enjoying his new status as Yale professor, traveling lecturer, and Republican elder statesman. He had dropped seventy-five pounds of excess weight through careful dieting. A reporter for the *New York Sun* in March found "the Taft smile as compelling, as engaging and as amiable as ever it was, however the frame of flesh about it has been lessened." The man himself was "happy and contented."[22]

As far as Taft's family affairs went, he had good reason to be pleased with his wife's recovery from her medical troubles in the White House. "Mrs. Taft is better now than she has been since her first attack in the White House," he told a friend on 9 July 1914. His eldest son Robert was starting his legal career in Cincinnati, where he continued the impressive intellectual talents he had displayed at Yale and the Harvard Law School. Helen Taft had returned to Bryn Mawr to finish out the college study that she had interrupted to help her mother during the presidency. Her father hoped she would pursue graduate work in English or history at Yale. The youngest child, Charles P. Taft, had gone through the Taft school to graduate at fifteen, had then studied with his uncle Horace for an additional year, and was planning to enter Yale in the fall of 1914. He would live with his fellow students because, as his father wrote, "It is not wise to have a boy live at home when he is at college."[23]

Taft had often reiterated that he had no political ambitions for seeking another office. However, he did want the Republican Party to regain power "to save the country from the sanctimonious opportunism of Wilson and the dangerous and reckless radicalism and demagogy of Roosevelt."[24] This meant thwarting any comeback attempt by Theodore Roosevelt. The year had not been kind to the Progressive Party or its leader. Those who had left the Republican ranks to support Roosevelt had drifted back toward the GOP as their own third party suffered a series of defeats in state and local elections. Roosevelt himself had made an ill-fated trip to South America where he had further impaired his health while exploring the jungles of the Amazon River. By the time Roosevelt returned to the United States in the spring, the political trends looked promising for the Republicans, difficult for the Democrats, and desperate for the Progressives. In Indiana, for example, Taft got reports that "Progressives are deserting the party" and that the Republicans "can possibly carry the state."

Taft got that political intelligence from former vice president Charles Warren Fairbanks when Taft came to Indiana to speak at the centennial of the New Harmony colony in early June. In a memoir that he drafted of the visit, Fairbanks concluded that "Mr. Taft, as the newspapers would say, was at his best." At a dinner in his honor, "there was nothing in his manner or speech to suggest that he is not the happiest man in America." Later he made another speech at New Harmony where "the impression made by Mr. Taft, both in his personal contact with the people and in his address upon the platform, was distinctly favorable."[25]

The sunny political prospects for the Republicans continued through much of the summer, which Taft spent with his family in the familiar haunts of Murray Bay, Canada. By late July, Taft realized with the rest of the United States that what had seemed unthinkable, a general war in Europe, was breaking out. He wrote "A Message to the People of the United States," which the *Independent* published in its issue of 10 August 1914. "It is a cataclysm. It is a retrograde step in Christian civilization," Taft remarked. "We have every reason to be happy that we are able to preserve strict neutrality in respect to it." The essay reflected Taft's disappointment that his optimistic hopes for world peace had been so shattered. "At the time when so many friends of peace have thought that we were making real progress toward the abolition of war this sudden outbreak of the greatest war in history is most discouraging. The future looks dark indeed, but we should not despair." Until the nations of the world came to their senses, there was little that Taft had to offer.[26]

Taft got the news about the war while he was in Canada and by September had made his way back to New Haven. Elihu Root teased him about his whereabouts. "I was glad to get your letter of September 2nd and to observe that you have returned to your natural habitat on Long Island Sound. I had begun to fear that you had been pressed into the Canadian contingent for the war in Europe and I thought we should never see you again, because if you got on the firing line it would just be impossible for the Germans to miss you."[27]

Personal kidding aside, Taft did not have an immediate answer to the emerging horror of the world conflict. When the Hearst newspaper chain invited him to become the head of a list of honorary members supporting Hearst's efforts "to work for peace in Europe," he declined. The better approach was to support the efforts of President Wilson as a mediator and to contribute to the efforts of the American Red Cross. As he told the editor of the *New York American*, "Such a committee at this time can accomplish practically nothing." For the moment, Taft continued with his legal and lecturing commitments and hoped for an Allied victory over Germany and its partners.[28]

One service that Taft rendered in this period was to sit on the committee that the National Association for the Advancement of Colored People (NAACP) had just established to award a medal (named for Joel Elias Spingarn) to the person who had done the most to advance the interests of black Americans. Taft suggested

Major Robert Russa Moton of the Hampton Normal and Agricultural Institute of Hampton, Virginia. The award went to another entrant, chemist Henry Just, but the work Taft did mitigated to a small degree his policies as president which had operated to limit the role of Afrian Americans within the Republican Party.[29]

On the other hand, Taft could be obtuse about the situation that ordinary black people confronted on a daily basis. To a correspondent who asked him about how blacks fared in the criminal justice system, he gave a platitudinous answer: "I have no doubt that a colored man receives a fair trial under the jury system in the United States, in every part of the country except where there is still an unreasoning prejudice against the race. I don't know how the injustice arising from racial prejudice can be eliminated in certain parts of the country." He believed that the lot of black people was improving and that, in time, "would give them a better chance for justice." To show that the Fifteenth Amendment "may not be palpably evaded by the states," he cited the recent Supreme Court decision outlawing the restrictive grandfather clause as a means of disenfranchising blacks. That was as far as former president Taft would go in 1915.[30]

When Booker T. Washington died in November 1915, Taft's comments to the press and in private struck the same note. Washington's death was "an irretrievable loss to the nation." Taft contended that Washington's "loving candor to his fellow negroes, his inspiring encouragement to make themselves individually valuable to the community, urging upon them the homely virtues of industry, thrift and persistent use of their opportunities, with a promise of higher achievements as a reward, have done more for the negro race than any other factor in their progress." Like so many other white politicians of that era, Taft did not often criticize whites for their role in the dire predicament that black people faced in the segregated nation.[31]

The personal highlight of the autumn of 1914 for Taft came with the meeting of the American Bar Association in Washington toward the end of October. At the suggestion of his reporter friend Gus Karger, Taft spoke to the National Press Club on 19 October as the organization moved into its new headquarters. "You are now an important and prosperous part of the community and therefore you are entitled to quarters of a magnificent and luxurious character, even if there is some difficulty in collecting the dues and meeting the rent. (Laughter)." He told the assembled scribes "the last fourteen or fifteen months that I have passed have really been, if not the happiest part of my life, certainly as happy as any other part that I have lived."[32]

As for the press itself, Taft said that "one of the things my life has given me an opportunity to study is the defects of newspapers (Laughter). It is a most delightful study. The conspiracies that are entered into of a world-wide character to keep people off the front page and relegate them to the eighteenth page, presents a tragedy that is most interesting to a man who has no place in any paper. (Laughter)." It was, said a Washington newspaper, "a characteristically happy little speech" that received "an enthusiastic reception" from the assembled reporters.[33]

The meeting of the American Bar Association two days later proved another success for Taft. His idea was to have attorneys from the United States, Canada, and Latin America come to Washington for the conclave. President Wilson addressed the membership with the justices of the Supreme Court in attendance. In his own address, Taft recalled the optimism of the previous meeting in Montreal when "there was nothing then in the world's horizon to trouble the friends of international peace." Now the nations of Europe were at war and the United States was neutral. Taft then endorsed the actions of the White House in the crisis. "The overwhelming importance to us of keeping out of the struggle has led President Wilson to warn the American people, in their public expressions and actions, to maintain, as far as possible, an impartial attitude, and in this appeal he should have the warmest approval and sincerest cooperation of us all."[34]

The main theme of Taft's address to his fellow lawyers was an examination of the antitrust and labor legislation that the Wilson presidency and the Congress had recently adopted in the Clayton Antitrust Act. The antitrust legislation contained language favorable to labor unions and their right to organize that, in Taft's words, "have been called the charter of liberty of labor." He found that actual change in the power of courts to issue injunctions in labor disputes was modest "compared with the very drastic and dangerous changes which were pressed and proclaimed as certain." He renewed his attacks on the doctrine of judicial recall as Theodore Roosevelt and the Progressive Party asserted it, but was pleased to report "that there has been a distinct falling off in support of these fundamentally unwise and dangerous proposals." Finally, he renewed a longtime proposal for the Congress to give the Supreme Court greater power to establish rules for handling cases involving civil actions in federal courts.[35]

Taft and his fellow Republicans had gone into the congressional elections of 1914 in hopes that Roosevelt and the Progressives would be repudiated and that the Democrats would suffer the anticipated losses in the first balloting after a presidential contest. The Republicans did bounce back from the debacle of 1912, but the gains did not achieve what they had sought in their most optimistic forecasts. The start of the war and the impulse to rally around the president in a foreign policy crisis helped the Democrats limit their setback. "With the war before their eyes," Gus Karger told Taft, "the people accept it as the cause of the evils which harass them."[36]

The voters did administer a severe rebuke to the Progressives and Theodore Roosevelt. With the intensity of 1912 absent, Republicans who had endorsed the third party drifted back to their partisan home. As a result, eight of the seventeen members of the House that the Progressives had elected in 1912 went down to defeat. There was a marked falloff in its national total to fewer than two million votes. Theodore Roosevelt conceded that "from Indiana eastward it is utterly impossible, if present conditions continue unchanged, that we shall again be able to make a serious fight."[37]

That outcome suited Taft very well. As he told Myron Herrick, the former ambassador to France, "Roosevelt was wiped out at the last election, and there is now no possibility of his leading the Republican party, or any other party to victory." With the gain of sixty-three Republican seats in the House, "Wilson's defeat in 1916 is as reasonably probable as any political event can be. The people of the country have turned their noses in that direction." In the aftermath of the enactment of the Underwood Tariff in 1913, there had been a loss of business confidence and a falloff in economic growth. Like other Republicans, Taft expected that the worsening economic conditions of 1914 would continue and propel the Grand Old Party back to the White House. He did not anticipate that war orders would restore prosperity and act as a boon to the president in his re-election bid.[38]

At the end of 1914, it had become evident that the war in Europe would be neither short nor decisive. Great Britain and France were locked into trench warfare with Germany, along hundreds of miles in the Belgian and French countryside, from the English Channel to the Swiss border. With winter affecting offensive operations, the attacks against the German lines had not yet started but would begin during the spring of 1915. The British had imposed a blockade on Germany, and Berlin was turning to the new weapon of submarine warfare to counter the naval tactics from London. A host of new issues pressed for resolution, including whether to commence increases in the American army and navy.

Taft resisted the clamor for immediate and extensive preparedness at the end of 1914. "The principle of common sense must be used in dealing with the proposed question of a larger army and navy," he told the Young Men's Christian Association of Brooklyn, New York, on 4 December 1914. Only when war came should the country "force men into the army or navy or take any action to that end or anything like that." Until actual fighting loomed, he favored some increases in the navy and building up the army to around 150,000 men, but no more than that. He opposed efforts, however, to ban the sale of munitions from the United States to the warring powers, which he understood would favor Germany against the Allies. In these views, Taft tracked the attitudes of most eastern Republicans during the first year of the fighting.[39]

Although he gained a reputation for both indolence and procrastination as president, Taft was in fact a man who enjoyed being busy, getting out on the road, and having favorite causes, such as the American Red Cross, that he could advance. One of his most important commitments after World War I began was the League to Enforce Peace, an organization that viewed concerted international action as the way to prevent future wars. Between 1915 and 1919, Taft was the most notable American political figure associated with the league, even though he was not a founder of the group, having come into its deliberations after the groundwork had been laid by others. By the spring of 1915, however, Taft had taken a leadership role in the league's public campaigns.

The origins of the League to Enforce Peace went back to the early days of the European war, when peace advocates in the United States sought ways in which to influence the way the world would function after the fighting had ended. The primary mover of this effort was Hamilton Holt, the publisher of the *Independent*, who had sponsored Taft's series of articles about world federation during the preceding spring. Holt had long proposed that the world community should emulate the United States and establish a rule of law among nations similar to the Constitution. He argued that force should be the ultimate weapon of nations allied to maintain the peace, a position that echoed what William Howard Taft believed. Just how the implementation of international force would operate was left for the future to decide.

Holt was a member of the New York Peace Society, which in the autumn of 1914 sponsored a small discussion meeting to ponder proposals to establish an international peace-keeping force through an association of nations. A "Plan of Action Committee" was formed, which met several times in the weeks that followed, leading up to a formal discussion by the Peace Society's executive committee in the last days of December. Talks continued through early 1915, when the Action Committee agreed to send out a report to all members of the Peace Society and begin a public campaign for an international peace force.

In the meantime, Holt and his allies began deliberating outside of the framework of the Peace Society, through a series of working dinners. One of the active participants was Theodore Marburg, who had been minister to Belgium during Taft's presidency. He sent information about the ongoing discussions regarding a "league of peace" to his former boss and arranged for Taft to lecture on the power of the presidency in April 1915. Marburg had been in communication with James Bryce, the former British ambassador to the United States, who was formulating his own "Proposals for the Prevention of Future Wars" at this time. These various currents came together at a third dinner meeting on 30 March 1915, where specific proposals for the League of Peace emerged. Since academics and intellectuals had been the major source of inspiration for the league up to that point, it was decided to present their ideas to more public figures ten days later on 9 April.

Taft attended that meeting and commented on the idea of first creating an international peace force to carry out the dictates of a tribunal to prevent wars. He differed with another one of the participants, A. Lawrence Lowell, the president of Harvard University, who endorsed force as a way of compelling nations to behave. As the talks proceeded, a consensus was reached on a set of resolutions that Taft agreed to edit for distribution to potential signers. Out of that process it was hoped that a league would emerge to press for the ideas that had been hashed over at the meeting.

In its broad outlines, the document tracked some of Taft's views. It urged the United States to become a member of a league that would submit justiciable questions to an international tribunal. United action by member nations would prevent a reliance on war before a judicial ruling could be achieved. In the event of disagreements not susceptible to judicial treatment, a council of conciliation would attempt to resolve differences. Finally, the participating countries would seek to codify rules of international law for the use of the tribunal.[40]

While the implementation of the resolutions adopted during the 9 April meeting went forward under Taft's auspices, a decisive event intervened that changed the shape of debate over American neutrality. On 7 May 1915, a German submarine torpedoed and sank the British ocean liner *Lusitania* off the Irish coast, with a loss of life that included more than 120 Americans on board. Subsequent

A. Lawrence Lowell. President of Harvard University, Lowell was a major Taft ally within the League to Enforce Peace. (Library of Congress LC-DIG-ggbain-06180)

tragedies of the twentieth century would come to overshadow the impact of the sinking of the *Lusitania,* but at the time it seemed to many Americans a war crime of immense proportions.

Because of the horrific nature of the loss of the ship, many Americans assumed that the United States would soon declare war on Germany. Theodore Roosevelt called it "not only an act of simple piracy" but something that "represented piracy accompanied by murder on a vaster scale than any old-time pirate had ever practiced before being hung for his misdeeds." Taft's former attorney general, George W. Wickersham, wrote a letter to the *New York Times* demanding action against Germany; he followed it up with an impassioned interview the next day. "The whole civilized world—and I take care to exclude Germany—looks to America to tell Germany where she stands as the avowed enemy of humanity and Christianity."[41]

These comments to the press did not impress Taft. He believed that Wickersham and Roosevelt "made asses of themselves and were most boyish in yielding to the passionate expressions that they uttered." Taft recalled his own difficult moments in the White House and "what an awful responsibility a man has to carry in such a crisis and how trying such blatherskiting is when a man is trying to find the right way out of a difficult situation."[42]

Unlike other Republicans, Taft had not made any personal attacks on Wilson's foreign policy in public. He saved his criticisms of what he regarded as the president's opportunism for private letters. These remarks do not seem to have made their way to Wilson, though he did not have much intellectual respect for his predecessor. Wilson had not appreciated Taft's strictures about his Philippine policy. That did not prevent the incumbent from receiving Taft at the White House when the former president came to Washington for events such as the American Bar Association meeting in October 1914.[43]

In the wake of the *Lusitania* crisis, Taft decided to write Wilson a general letter of support "to express, in a deeply sympathetic way, my appreciation of the difficult situation which you face. It seems to me that it is the duty of every thoughtful, private citizen to avoid embarrassing you in your judgment and not to yield to the impulse of deep indignation which the circumstances naturally arouse, and demand at once a resort to extreme measures which mean war." Taft suggested a possible break in diplomatic relations with Germany if Berlin's response to protests about the sinking of the liner proved unsatisfactory. He also mentioned summoning Congress for further action. He assured Wilson that "you have able Counsellors about you" who knew more of the international situation than Taft did. They might differ from what the former president advised, but he wanted to tell Wilson of "my confidence that you will take the wise and patriotic course and that you will avoid war, if it is possible."[44]

Wilson responded with warm thanks to Taft's missive. "I think the whole country admires, as I do, the generous spirit in which you have sunk all considerations of party and have come to my support at this critical juncture in our history." The president did not share any substantive plans he had for dealing with the crisis. He was probably less than impressed with what Taft had to offer. The suggestions that Taft made differed only in timing from what Roosevelt and Wickersham had proposed with more heat. Breaking diplomatic relations, which would have meant war, remained an option for Wilson, but not something he wanted to do except as a last resort in the face of German intransigence. In the meantime, he sought to negotiate with Berlin about an acceptable resolution.[45]

Taft circulated his letter and Wilson's reply to friends such as Gus Karger and others. He provided public support to the White House in a speech to the Union League Club of Philadelphia on 11 May, the day after his letter went to the president. "The task of the President is a heavy one. He is our President. He is acting for the whole country. He is anxious to find a way out of the present difficulty without war." He advocated standing by Wilson as he grappled with the crisis. Taft had written his remarks on the way to Philadelphia and "was a little uncertain whether I ought to deliver it or not, but on the whole concluded to let it go."[46]

One element in Taft's thinking about his relations with Wilson at this time may well have been his increasing commitment to the fortunes of the League to Enforce Peace. With his background in political campaigns, including two presidential races, Taft offered his colleagues in the peace effort some practical ideas on how to generate public support. He collaborated with William Harrison Short of the New York Peace Society in sending out letters to prominent individuals asking them to join the new organization. In late May, with Taft taking the lead, a committee of one hundred individuals announced a conference to be held in Philadelphia on 17 June to form a "League of Peace or League of Nations."[47]

The call for meeting contained the text that Taft had worked out in April. Newspapers noted that the Wilson administration was not sending any official representative to the gathering. Reporters asked Wilson at a news conference on 8 June if the government had offered any encouragement to the meeting. "No, sir. We haven't had anything to do with it one way or the other. I didn't ask for our [participation]." The president very much wanted to keep diplomacy in his own hands and intended to maintain at least an arm's-length approach to the league and its activities.[48]

At the 17 June meeting, which happened to coincide with the centennial of the Battle of Waterloo, Taft could only be present for part of the deliberations. "We are in favor of doing something as well as thinking something. I believe in praying for peace and I also believe in doing something to support that prayer." The delegates adopted the proposals as written by Taft and A. Lawrence Lowell, and elected Taft as president of the League to Enforce Peace, American Branch. Delegates laid plans to establish a permanent structure for the new league on 29 June.[49]

While Wilson had not endorsed the league and would remain aloof from it for the next year, he and Taft had maintained an air of public cooperation and civility on foreign affairs that contrasted with the vehement assaults on the White House from Theodore Roosevelt. Neither Wilson nor Taft really respected each other as politicians and statesmen, but each had good incentives to give an impression of comity and mutual support. Such an alliance could not endure very long, given the pressures working on each man as the 1916 election approached. For Taft, he had to keep his lines open to the Republican presidential candidates. If Wilson lost and a Supreme Court vacancy opened up, Taft would want to have his partisan credentials in order for a new Republican chief executive.

One constant in Taft's postpresidential life through mid-1915 was the continuation of his bitterness toward Theodore Roosevelt. The two men came together for the first time in April 1915 at the funeral of a deceased professor at Yale, Thomas A. Lounsbury. Each had been invited to serve as an honorary pallbearer for the departed academic. Elaborate preparations made sure that the former friends rode in separate vehicles and had only the most minimal exposure to each other. They exchanged pleasantries about their families and that was the end of the occasion. Taft found Roosevelt "not looking especially well."[50]

That spring, a Republican politician in New York State, William Barnes, sued Roosevelt for libel. Roosevelt had called Barnes a political boss among Republicans in the state, and a trial ensued in Syracuse. The litigation became a sensation as the newspapers re-examined Roosevelt's political career. The jury found for Roosevelt in proceedings that left Taft frustrated over the rulings of the trial judge, "who allowed a lot of matters to get before the jury that had no real relations to the case." The successful outcome of the case for Roosevelt, Taft believed, would not help the former president return to Republican politics, because "he does not know the abysmal depths that he has reached in the opinion of the men who are likely to control the Republican Convention and Republican politics in the next Presidential campaign."[51]

While Roosevelt and his ambitions would continue as a potential menace to the revival of Republican fortunes and the ouster of Wilson from the White House as 1916 loomed, Taft saw the war as the main element shaping American affairs in the spring of 1915. "War is a dreadful thing, and I don't know when we are going to finish it," he wrote to his elderly aunt Delia Torrey in mid-June. The accumulated problems of the American Red Cross, the League to Enforce Peace, and the Philippines, along with the question of Wilson's re-election, made the remainder of 1915 a period that tested Taft's political commitments.[52]

3

STRAINS IN THE TAFT-WILSON
RELATIONSHIP, 1915–1916

After his vigorous spring of lecturing and involvement with the origins of the League to Enforce Peace, William Howard Taft looked forward, as he did every year with the approach of summer, to getting away to his Canadian retreat at Murray Bay, Quebec. "I am longing to get away for Murray Bay," he wrote to his brother Horace on 22 June 1915. Will and Nellie had first visited the small village on the St. Lawrence River in 1892, and decided right then to make it their summer residence away from the heat, first of Cincinnati and later of Washington, D.C.[1]

Over the next two decades, the emotional, residential, and financial commitment to the Canadian community deepened for the Tafts. They resided at Fassifern Cottage, a dwelling they expanded into a sprawling complex that included some twenty bedrooms and twelve bathrooms. The burgeoning Taft family and their friends from Cincinnati came to a building that featured flags and mementoes from the former president's service in the Philippines. In time there even developed a Taft family anthem to mark the presence of the clan at Murray Bay:

Once there was a president whose name was William Taft
He came to La Malbaie on a great big river raft
And when he saw the Pointe au Pic
He said "that's one for me,
I'll go ashore and build a house and raise a family."

Fat Tafts, thin Tafts, any Tafts at all
Come to the Manning house and have yourselves a ball.
Be sure to park your rods and your golf clubs at the door
And you'll hear such caterwauling as you never heard before.

Will became very much involved in the affairs of his summer hideaway. The locals dubbed him "the little Judge" in a somewhat ironic fashion. Because it was in Canada and thus outside the boundaries of the United States, Murray Bay had been off-limits to Taft during his presidency. He and his wife had to settle for Beverly, Massachusetts, which had never approached the amenities and atmosphere of the St. Lawrence landscape and climate. When he was able to return to Canada in July 1913, "the wealth of memory and enjoyment is great." From the heat of New York on a train trip to Montreal, the Tafts were soon sleeping "under a blanket." The change, he wrote to Horace, "is calculated to restore spirits, give you an appetite, promote somnolence, reconcile you to Democratic government, make you considerate of Roosevelt and accomplish any heretofore impossible task."[2]

The most important feature of Murray Bay from Taft's perspective was the proximity to a golf course. Ever since taking up the game two decades earlier, he had devoted most of his leisure hours in pursuit of lower scores and victories over his playing partners. "It has been cold and rainy since we have been here," he reported to Gus Karger on 3 July 1915, "but I have been able to play golf every day." In the afternoons, he worked on legal matters, wrote lectures (which he called "a great bore" that had to be done), and welcomed relatives and friends to the resort. When he had all the guests their remodeled house could handle, Taft was "delighted because there is nothing pleasanter to me than a house full of guests."[3]

One of the legal matters that Taft worked on during the summer of 1915 involved an advisory opinion on a pending legal case arising out of the troubled affairs of the Rock Island Railroad and its receivers. Although he maintained his stance of not appearing before judges in federal courts or engaging in ordinary litigation, he believed that it was appropriate for him to offer advisory opinions, for a fee, in selected cases. One such proceeding during the summer of 1915 dealt with the Chicago, Rock Island, and Pacific Railroad, and charges that its board of directors had misappropriated funds. The receivers for the troubled line included Jacob M. Dickinson, who had been secretary of war for the first two years of Taft's presidency. When the trial judge asked Dickinson to have a distinguished attorney look into the facts of the litigation, he knew just where to turn.

Dickinson asked Taft to prepare an advisory opinion on the legality of what the railroad had been doing with its assets. Taft responded with a lengthy document, to which his son Robert had made an important contribution, indicating that the receivers should take action against the directors over their misuse of funds. A federal judge agreed with Taft's views in the case and ordered the receivers to bring suit against the previous management. The disclosure of Taft's actions in the opinion came, in the words of one newspaper, as "a distinct surprise."[4]

Taft remained in the public eye in the United States even while he was in Canada. The *Saturday Evening Post* of 5 June 1915 carried his opinion piece on the current controversy about national defense. He doubted whether the nation would pay for a volunteer army of half a million men in peacetime, or that volunteers would fill the ranks in time of war. He discussed the logistical difficulties that both the army and navy confronted and urged that both services should be enhanced to some degree. "There is no occasion for alarm," he concluded. "Indeed I think alarmist articles weaken the force of the argument in favor of reasonable preparedness." Modest increases in military expenditures would provide the muscle for a League to Enforce Peace. "We shall be much more influential in leading the other nations into such a League if we are in a state of proper national defense."[5]

The outbreak of World War I had given new impetus to the work of the American Red Cross and posed fresh challenges to the relationship between Taft and Mabel Boardman. The Red Cross sent thirteen hospital units to the fighting fronts in Europe at the end of 1914, and more followed during the early part of 1915. An initial surge in donations sustained the Red Cross effort in this opening phase of the war, though as Boardman reported to Taft, "one thing that has hurt us is the numerous other committees appealing for funds. I have learned today of two more, making thirty-four in all."[6]

As the war expanded, so did the work of the Red Cross, but the initial surge of donations ebbed away. By the summer of 1915, the money had become so scarce that the organization announced in June that the hospital units would be withdrawn from the fighting areas "because of a lack of funds to maintain them longer at their stations." These developments convinced Taft to make a change in the leadership of the organization even if it meant a diminished role for his friend Mabel Boardman. Despite his regard for her as a person and leader of the Red Cross, he did not believe that a woman could be an effective leader of the organization during the wartime crisis. The death of her father in August 1915 added to Taft's sense that she needed assistance with the management of the organization.[7]

President Wilson asked Taft in late October to become chair of the Central Committee of the Red Cross. Details would be worked out at a meeting of the panel in early December. Taft told Mabel Boardman that he would accept the post "on one condition, my dear Mabel, and that is that you are to let go." While he had sincere concern for his close friend, his urging that she cut back on her commitment to the Red Cross also allowed men to take a greater part in the management of the charitable organization.[8]

When the president and Taft met in early December in Washington to set the Red Cross on a new course, they had the group adopt new bylaws that created "the department of military relief and the department of civilian relief, each under a director general." Taft enlisted a former general to direct the daily operation of the Red Cross. Boardman fought back against these bureaucratic changes, but her position, once so powerful in the Red Cross, never recovered from the changes that her friend Will Taft had put into motion in late 1915.[9]

The summer stay at Murray Bay in 1915 was shorter than Taft would have liked. He had committed himself to an extensive lecture tour that took him across the country in August and September, ending in California at the Pan-Pacific Exposition. In addition to the article on the state of the nation's defenses for the *Saturday Evening Post,* he worked on another for the same journal about women's suffrage, which Taft opposed. He did not believe that women were interested in politics and he feared that unqualified female voters would outweigh more knowledgeable women at the polls.

With the 1916 presidential election still a year away, "Republican politics are very dead for the time being." Looking at the prospects, he concluded that "if the war continues and the present situation is maintained, it seems to me that Wilson is likely to be returned, and I don't see any prospect of the war ending for two more years. It is horrible to think what the exhaustion will be."[10]

While he had praised the president over the handling of the *Lusitania* controversy and had courted the White House over the approach of the League to Enforce Peace, Taft had remained skeptical in public and private over the treatment of the Philippines. He had on several occasions during 1915 reiterated his pessimistic view of the capabilities of the Filipinos to govern themselves without American tutelage. Before a Senate committee in January 1915, he estimated "that it will take more than one generation, and probably two, if you count a generation as 30 years" before the people of the island would be ready to run their country without supervision.[11]

Opponents of Wilson's Philippine policy made sure that Taft received ample inside information about Burton Harrison's changes to the political arrangements in the archipelago. In March 1915, addressing the National Geographic Society in Washington, Taft argued that the Democratic regime had "cost millions of pesos more than necessary." Reporters asked Wilson about Taft's comments at his next news conference on 30 March, and the president responded, "I hope when I get out of office my successors will not express an opinion with regard to what I said about them." He went on to say that he did not think the incumbent chief executive should respond to what his predecessor was saying about him. There was a certain touchiness about the episode that indicated the president's continuing sensitivity to Taft's criticisms.[12]

Because of his proprietary attitude toward his time in the Philippines, Taft could not leave the topic alone. The shift in policy toward more immediate promises of Philippine independence from the Democrats seemed an indictment of his performance both as governor general and as president. He felt impelled to make the Republican case against what the administration was doing. Francis Harrison told the White House that Taft "with his usual gullibility, allowed himself to be made the mouthpiece" for partisan attacks on the Democratic policy in the islands. According to the governor general, the Republican assaults had been failing, but he expected that a renewed effort to indict his regime for "destroying efficiency" would be mounted. Thus the resumption of Taft's campaign on the Philippines came as fulfillment of these expectations.[13]

When the former president departed for the West Coast in August, he had already drafted a speech about the handling of Mexico and the Philippines that he delivered to the Commonwealth Club of California on 6 September 1915. To his audience, Taft asserted that Harrison was "a Tammany Congressman of long standing" who had joined with Manuelo Quezon, "a Filipino politician of not the highest standing in the Philippines." They had removed American officials dedicated to efficiency to appoint in their place less qualified Filipinos.[14]

The Democrats were pushing a measure called the Jones Bill, named after Representative William A. Jones of Virginia, which promised the Filipinos eventual independence when a workable government existed, and in the meantime greater autonomy in most of their domestic affairs. No specific timetable was set, and Taft therefore regarded the Jones bill as a cynical measure. "What's the use of fooling the Filipinos by such a declaration?" he asked in San Francisco.[15] The Republicans had blocked the Jones legislation at the end of the previous session of Congress, but it was going to be considered again when lawmakers assembled in December. The White House also believed that the Republicans were going to make the fate of the Philippines a major issue in the forthcoming presidential election.

To Taft's strictures, the administration responded that their policy in the islands was "Filipinization," and they rejected the allegations that a spoils system existed. The former president's comments were old and tired, said an official at the War Department, who was probably Secretary Lindley M. Garrison. The removal of American officials and the appointment of Filipinos to positions of responsibility was a way of testing whether the people of the archipelago were indeed ready for self-government and eventual independence.[16]

The controversy over the Philippines erupted two months later when a Republican member of the House of Representatives, Clarence Miller of Minnesota, returned from a trip to the islands to say that under Harrison and the Democrats the Filipinos had received "the worst possible government." Taft echoed Miller's charges in November when he told an interviewer in Chicago for the *New York Times* that the Filipino people were still two generations away from being ready to govern themselves. "The laborious effort of fourteen years has been practically destroyed. Its restoration now would be a matter of extreme difficulty." In these weeks, Taft also wrote an introduction for a volume attacking the Democratic record in the Philippines, an action that irked Secretary Garrison and his aides.[17]

Garrison saw Taft's tactics as partisan and unfair, and he decided, without consulting the White House, to launch a direct public challenge to the former president. The War Department had information that they thought would embarrass Taft and reveal his partisan motivations in criticizing Harrison and the Philippine policy. The release of the statement damaging to Taft came right after the Thanksgiving holiday with the aim of receiving maximum publicity. The attack on the former president succeeded in attracting widespread newspaper coverage but did not work out to discredit him as Garrison had planned.

According to the statement that Garrison distributed to the press on 29 November 1915, O. Garfield Jones had also been in touch with the War Department about the Philippines. He revealed in a letter of 28 October that he had indeed written an "anti-administration"

Lindley M. Garrison. Secretary of War in the early years of the Wilson administration, Garrison carried on a public feud with Taft over Philippine policy. (Library of Congress LC-USZ62-100793)

article for the *Oakland Tribune* at the behest of Francis B. Loomis, a former Republican diplomat. But, he told the War Department, he had an equal amount of positive material about Harrison's work in the Philippines that he would be glad to write for a newspaper friendly to the White House. "Will you please give me a list of the three or four big newspapers that are most pro-Wilson and are likely to want pro-administration articles on the P. I's?"[18]

Garrison alleged that what Jones had written and Taft had supported was in fact a fabrication that undercut all of his criticisms of the Wilson policies toward the archipelago. At the end of his statement, the secretary of war adopted a condescending tone toward Taft: "A sickening sense of shame must overcome Mr. Taft when he realizes where his blind partisanship in this matter has led him."[19]

If the secretary of war expected Taft to issue an apology for his criticism of the president's policy or the endorsement of the Jones articles, he soon learned otherwise. The former president explained that he had seen in manuscript what Jones had written during his stay in San Francisco in September. Since the reporter's critique echoed what Taft had been hearing about the Philippines from other sources, he wrote an introduction in which he said that "the policy of the present administration will drive every self-respecting American from the islands if continued for any great length of time." In his rebuttal to Garrison in late November, Taft added that "I have not been unmindful of the necessity for standing by this Democratic administration in national crisis, without regard to party considerations."[20]

In private, Taft concluded that Jones "seems to have been a good deal of a fool and a good deal of a knave." The *New York Sun* called him "readily reversible." Nonetheless, Secretary Garrison returned to the controversy on 1 December, stating: "What I said concerning Mr. Taft was absolutely just, was less vehement than the circumstances warranted, and I measured every word of it." The former president fired back: "Mr. Garrison's defense of the Harrison regime in the islands when the truth permeates the local atmosphere will only awaken ridicule and surprise that he could so deceive himself."[21]

As Taft dealt in public with the opportunistic record of his source, he was once again on more familiar ground in his critique of the underlying policy toward the Philippines. In the back and forth with Garrison over that subject, Taft's responses had a positive impact on the press and gave the former president the advantage in the controversy. Gus Karger reported doubts at the White House "whether Mr. Garrison evoked administration applause." Joe Tumulty, the president's secretary, told Karger in confidence, "I think he made a terrible mistake." Tumulty attributed Garrison's approach to "a greatly enlarged and swollen head."[22]

The Philippine issue between Garrison and Taft sputtered to an end in early 1916 as national defense preparedness and other questions emerged with the convening of Congress. The resignation of Garrison from the War Department in early 1916 removed one of the key critics of Taft's public stance on the islands. Wilson endorsed the Jones Bill, which created a legislature for the islands and also contained a firm promise to leave once the Philippines had a stable government. Elaborate legislative maneuvering went on through 1916, finally culminating with the passage of the Jones Act in August 1916. Writing about the record of the administration for the 1916 Republican campaign, Taft predicted that with enactment of the Jones measure, "we shall again have to do the work which we once did in restoring peace and tranquility to the islands. The Philippines will otherwise become another Mexico."[23]

American entry into World War I in 1917 allowed the Philippine issue to recede from the forefront of foreign policy issues for the next four years. In 1918, the former president felt some sense of vindication when Harrison's second wife filed for divorce. "He is a skunk, I believe," Taft wrote his wife. When Taft revisited the problem in February 1921 at the onset of the administration of Warren G. Harding, he remained critical of Harrison and what the Democrats had done. He recognized that there was no going back to the kind of imperial tutelage he had practiced two decades earlier. "The American people are not prepared to make the sacrifice," he wrote. All he could recommend was that the new administration consider the problem with care.[24]

Taft's campaign against Wilson over the Philippines had thus ended in failure by 1916. If it had no effect on the president's policy, it did represent a source of strain between the two men that has not yet been assessed in understanding their political relationship. Wilson saw Taft as an unrepentant partisan who lacked sound judgment. In later crises over foreign policy, the president would have serious reservations and credible doubts about his predecessor's ability to rise above his Republican allegiance.

The early weeks of 1916 produced another area of intense contention between Taft and the president. On 2 January one of Taft's appointees to the Supreme Court, Joseph Rucker Lamar, died after only a few years on the bench. During the first two years of the post-presidency, there had been occasional speculation that Wilson might name Taft to the court when a vacancy occurred. But this was never more than newspaper gossip, since the chance of the first Democratic president in fifteen years choosing his predecessor for the court was close to zero.

In January 1914, newspaper reports circulated that Chief Justice Edward D. White might retire and Taft take his place. To a correspondent who wrote him about such stories, Taft replied: "It is absurd to suppose Chief Justice White, in the very acme of his usefulness, strength and power should be thinking of retiring and it is also absurd to suppose that President Wilson would not find in his own party a gentleman he thinks fitted for the place." To his former secretary of war Jacob M. Dickinson, he wrote, "The suggestion that he would appoint me is ridiculous."[25]

Wilson's first appointment was James C. McReynolds, who turned out to be very conservative once on the court. The president was not about to make that mistake again. While there was, once more, newspaper speculation about a Taft appointment, Wilson was soon prepared to move in what proved to be a much more controversial direction. Acting on the suggestion of several close aides, the president looked to Louis D. Brandeis of Boston, known as the "People's Lawyer" for his espousal of various progressive causes. On 28 January, Wilson sent the nomination of Brandeis to the Senate. Progressives exulted. "The appointment of Brandeis was the biggest of all the big things this administration has done for the American people," said one happy Texas Democrat. When reporters reached Taft during a trip to Trenton, New Jersey, he said only: "I have no comment to make." [26]

Of all the Supreme Court selections Woodrow Wilson might have made, the choice of Louis D. Brandeis was the most offensive to William Howard Taft. The two men had been involved in one of the signal episodes of the Taft presidency, the Ballinger-Pinchot controversy over conservation in 1909–1911. In the public relations struggle for advantage in that battle, Brandeis had embarrassed the president and suggested that the chief executive had been underhanded and duplicitous. It was a charge that stung the sensitive Taft and he had not forgotten what had happened six years later.

In the summer of 1909, a government investigator named Louis R. Glavis had charged that Secretary of the Interior Richard A. Ballinger had misused his office on behalf of claimants to lucrative coal lands in Alaska. Chief Forester Gifford Pinchot, who was feuding with Ballinger, had Glavis send his charges to the president. Taft had received the allegations, met with Glavis, and then prepared a response in consultation with Ballinger and Attorney General George W. Wickersham. Taft and Wickersham decided to have the attorney general pull together a report that would be backdated to indicate that the president had relied on "his summary of the evidence and his conclusions therefrom." This kind of bureaucratic procedure was not new to the practice of government, but it left the two men open to a charge of seeking to mislead the public.[27]

In the months that followed, the controversy between Pinchot and Ballinger became hotter. *Collier's Magazine* published an article detailing the Glavis charges. A public scandal erupted in which Pinchot issued serious claims of wrongdoing. Taft fired Pinchot in January 1910, a move that became a turning point in the president's worsening relations with Theodore Roosevelt. A congressional investigation ensued in which Louis D. Brandeis represented the interest of *Collier's* and by extension Gifford Pinchot. As the facts developed, however, it became clearer that many of the allegations against Ballinger were overstated and not sustainable.

Louis D. Brandeis. Taft became a strident public opponent of the nomination of Brandeis to the Supreme Court in 1916. (Library of Congress LC-DIG-ggbain-2100)

With his legal acumen, Brandeis wondered how the attorney general had been able to master the extensive record of the Glavis charges and write a detailed report within the two-day time frame that President Taft's documents had specified. The answer of course was that he had not in fact done so, and the dating of the documents was not credible. Brandeis released charges of presidential wrongdoing in the incident. The resulting furor compelled the White House and the president to admit the backdating of the documents in an embarrassing episode. The attempt to cover up this bureaucratic shuffle seemed to validate Brandeis's overall case against the White House. Brandeis had prevailed and Taft appeared to be duplicitous and less than candid. For a man as concerned about his personal honor as Taft was, it was a public slight that he never forgot. His grievance showed up in a small way when he struck Brandeis twice from the list of committee assignments for the American Bar Association, once he became president of that body in 1913.[28]

Theodore Roosevelt once observed to his military aide, Archie Butt, that "Mr. Taft was one of the best haters he had ever known," who "does not easily forgive." Lacking political self-awareness, Taft never understood that he had created his own predicament in the Ballinger matter that Brandeis had exploited. It would have been better for him to have learned from the experience and chalked it up to the vagaries of the Washington way of doing things. Instead, he nursed a lasting grievance against Brandeis that now emerged to drive his reaction to the Supreme Court appointment.[29]

An undercurrent of anti-Semitism accounted for much of the opposition to the Brandeis nomination. That noxious sentiment did not animate William Howard Taft in his reaction to the president's selection. During his presidency, Taft had criticized a Washington club for blackballing a Jewish member. He had also taken up the case of a Jewish military officer who encountered bigotry. In public statements, he had praised the contribution of Jews in American history and criticized the repressive reaction of the tsarist regime in Russia for its pogroms against its Jewish citizens. He continued to utter such sentiments in the years after the White House. "The Jews in Russia and Poland have my profound sympathy," he wrote in March 1916, at the height of the Brandeis controversy, and he added that "the Jews of America have been among our most intelligent, enterprising, and patriotic citizens."[30]

On occasion, Taft could slip into the language of stereotypes. In October 1916, he told his brother Charles and his wife Annie that he and she would be encountering Colonel Isaac Ullman and his wife when the Tafts and their party from New Haven visited the birthplace of Revolutionary War hero Nathan Hale. "At first sight, Annie will be troubled by the appearance of Mrs. Ullman, and perhaps with the Colonel. The Hebrew marks in their faces, and in Mrs. Ullman's rather loud tones are unmistakable, but Ullman is one of the whitest men I know, and his wife is, under a somewhat unfortunate manner and exterior, a very good and fine woman."[31]

These occasional rhetorical lapses aside, Taft was less inclined to anti-Semitism than many of his political colleagues. His disapproval of Brandeis sprang from ideological differences and a visceral dislike of how the Supreme Court nominee had conducted himself as an attorney. On 31 January, three days after the selection was made, he told Gus Karger that "it is one of the deepest wounds that I have had as an American and a lover of the Constitution and a believer in progressive conservatism, that a man such as Brandeis could be put on the Court, as I believe he is likely to be." For Taft the personal and professional qualities that Brandeis had displayed made him unsuited to be a Supreme Court justice:

He is a muckraker, an emotionalist for his own purposes,
a socialist, prompted by jealousy, a hypocrite, a
man who has certain high ideals in his imagination,
but who is utterly unscrupulous in method of reaching
them, a man of infinite cunning, of marked ability
in that direction that hardly rises above the dignity
of cunning, of great tenacity of purpose, and, in my
judgment, of much power for evil.[32]

At the same time, Taft believed that Brandeis was insincere in his espousal of the cause of Zionism and a homeland in the Middle

East for the Jews. Brandeis had been mentioned for a cabinet post under Wilson in 1912 and 1913 but had run afoul of conservatives and, according to Taft, "leading Jews" who "advised Wilson that he was not a representative Jew." In Taft's mind, Brandeis then "became a Jew of the Jews after that, a Zionist, a new Jerusalemist, was metaphorically circumcised again, spent his time addressing Jews in every city in the country, wearing his hat and out Jewing the Rabbis of all but the most bearded orthodox of the Sanhedrin. It has worked to a charm."[33]

Taft's interpretation hardly did justice to the sincere commitment that Brandeis made to the cause of Zionism after 1913. Had his language to his brother become public knowledge, it would have cast a shadow on his motivation and attitudes. He did not include such allegations in his letter to Gus Karger, himself Jewish, but saved them for members of his immediate family. By 1916, Taft was ready to adopt almost any credible negative criticism of Brandeis as his own.

Taft believed that the Brandeis appointment showed President Wilson's true nature as a political intriguer and would in time work against him. "This appointment will be remembered long after the excitement of the confirmation has passed away, and it will return to plague him, as it ought to." Noting that he had been suggested as a replacement for Justice Lamar, Taft concluded: "When you consider Brandeis' appointment, and think that men were pressing me for the place, *es ist zum lachen.*"[34] In other words, "it's laughable."

From the beginning of the Brandeis controversy, Taft expected that the nomination would be confirmed. The Democrats had a strong majority in the Senate, and several progressive Republican members were likely to vote for Brandeis as well. So controversial was the nomination that the Senate held hearings on the legal record of the nominee. Gus Karger kept Taft informed on the progress of the hearings into Brandeis and his qualifications. The Senate committee handling the hearings was sympathetic to Brandeis. Therefore, concluded Karger, "unless something of unquestionable character is brought out, the public generally will look upon it as a mere difference of opinion with regard to the ethics of the profession, lacking easily understood questions of conscience or character."[35]

As the hearings unfolded, Karger's forecast proved accurate. The testimony showed that Brandeis was an effective lawyer who sometimes displayed sharp elbows in and out of court. When the hearings paused in early March, Karger told Taft that "if the testimony there adduced had concerned Elihu Root, friend of the corporations, today he would be denounced from coast to coast and his associates would seek to disbar him; it's different in the case of Louis D. Brandeis, friend of the people." Karger's tone indicated that the hearings had not produced any revelations that would doom the nomination.[36]

Taft could read the senatorial signs as well, and he had conceded that his political enemy was probably going to be confirmed. He decided at that point in the controversy that he needed to speak out in the most effective manner possible to at least go on record in person against Brandeis. What better means of criticism than to use his standing and the reputation of other lawyers as former presidents of the prestigious American Bar Association.

Working with Austen G. Fox, the New York attorney leading the anti-Brandeis forces, Taft wrote a brief letter that said "the undersigned feel under a painful duty to say to you that in their opinion, taking into view the reputation, character, and professional career of Mr. Louis D. Brandeis, he is not a fit person to be a member of the Supreme Court of the United States." He then circulated it to several former presidents of the American Bar Association for their signatures. His hope was that such men "were sufficiently representative of the American Bar to make the protest seem a weighty one." The letter gained the support of Elihu Root, Joseph Hodges Choate, and Moorfield Storey, as well as three other former ABA presidents.[37]

Austen Fox submitted the letter to the Senate committee dealing with the Brandeis nomination on 14 March 1916, and the newspapers covered the release of the document amid the other actions of the Senate Judiciary subcommittee on that day. The editors of the *Washington Times* called it "almost unthinkable" that the Senate would "in defiance of the protests of the most eminent members of the American Bar Association" decide to elevate Brandeis to the court. "If it does, it will be the darkest scandal ever suffered by the Supreme Court in all its history."[38]

Taft knew that his public protest against Brandeis would revive the controversy over the Ballinger-Pinchot episode. He did not have to wait long for what he called "the muckraking machine" to respond to his letter. Four days later Walter Lippmann in the *New Republic* reminded his readers that Taft's handling of the back-dated letter in 1909 represented "what is perhaps the most deplorable episode in which a President of the United States has been involved." Brandeis, Lippmann went on, had "demonstrated to the country Mr. Taft's immoral procedure in a disreputable incident." The reformer Florence Kelley also weighed in against Taft in the March 1916 issue of the *Survey*. The progressive columnist Gilson Gardner, spurred on by the urgings of activist and Brandeis supporter George Rublee, circulated a column about "Taft's Personal Grievance against Brandeis."[39]

Lippmann's editorial so outraged Taft that he contemplated suing the journal for libel. He relished the idea of being able to "try out the matter and inflict a substantial verdict on the entire contingent running the magazine." George Wickersham and his brother Henry, a New York attorney, persuaded him not to dignify the allegations of the *New Republic* with the free publicity that the suit would provide. "The paragraph in the *New Republic* is vicious and abominable. But it won't hurt you one whit, and unless made the subject of a law suit few will see it and still fewer be impressed with anything but disgust at it."[40]

Taft's protest had no effect on the progress of the Brandeis nomination. There were more twists and turns not involving Taft before the Senate acted in Brandeis's favor. With strong backing from President Wilson, the nominee was eventually confirmed on 1 June 1916. Taft had to accept the result he had long dreaded. Given his political and legal animus against Brandeis, it was inevitable that the former president would involve himself in the confirmation struggle in some manner.

Taft would have done better to have kept himself aloof from the struggle. The letter he devised for the former presidents of the American Bar Association (ABA) to sign rested in the end on the prestige of their opposition to the nominee. Taft did not believe he had to make an intellectual case against Brandeis as an attorney and Supreme Court nominee. He did not delve into the record that the Senate committee was compiling and thus did not have a command of the allegations for and against Brandeis. Convinced that his word as a former president of the ABA would be sufficient on its own, Taft did enough to indicate his prejudice against Wilson's selection without offering a rationale for opposition.

What Taft wrote represented the general feeling among conservative lawyers that Brandeis as an attorney was not to be trusted. As one of his colleagues in Boston remarked, Brandeis "fights to win, and fights up to the limits of his rights with a stern and even cruel exultation in the defeat of his adversary." A difference of legal style, however unwelcome to William Howard Taft, offered a weak foundation for the rejection of a Supreme Court nominee. While he did study the record of the Judiciary Committee hearings after he had made his protest, Taft's feelings about Brandeis were content-free in terms of specific negative allegations and very emotional. It was far from his best moment as an attorney and former occupant of the White House.[41]

The Brandeis battle left Taft even more disillusioned with President Wilson as a political leader. That posed a problem considering that he wanted Wilson to endorse his pet peace program. Taft in the spring of 1916 hoped to persuade the president to attend the first annual meeting of the League to Enforce Peace, scheduled for the end of May in Washington. Taft wrote to Wilson on 11 April 1916 to invite him to speak at the League's banquet on Saturday 27 May. Taft noted that Wilson had earlier in the year—in Des Moines, Iowa—said, "I pray to God that if this contest have no other result, it will at least have the result of creating an international tribunal and producing some sort of joint guaranty of peace on the part of the great nations of the world."[42]

Using this remark as a hook for the president, Taft argued that the

League assembly "offers the most favorable occasion to secure the close attention which we desire for the expression and expansion of the keynote you struck so aptly in the phrase I have quoted." Wilson responded three days later that it was "practically impossible for me to prepare an address nowadays and I have no choice but to hope merely that some other way may disclose itself in which I can show my earnest sympathy with the cause of organized peace."[43]

When Wilson wrote to Taft, he and the nation were in the midst of another submarine crisis arising from the torpedoing of the English Channel steamer, the *Sussex*, on 24 March 1916. Intense negotiations with Germany about the action of their submarines continued during April, with the risk of war on everyone's mind. In a speech at the Mystic Club in Chicago on 21 April, Taft told the audience that what Wilson was demanding of Germany in the way of a pledge not to repeat the policy that had brought on the crisis was correct. "In view of the critical nature of the issue," he asked his listeners, "is there anything for a clear-headed patriotic American to do but to back up our President who is our chosen constitutional leader?" Wilson wrote him: "I am sure you must instinctively know how warmly I appreciate your attitude in the present crisis, but I want to give myself the pleasure of sending you at least this line of appreciation."[44]

Taft renewed the invitation for the president to address the League to Enforce Peace on 9 May. There was no immediate response, but on 18 May the president sent a letter in a more receptive mood. "I am hoping with a good deal of confidence that it will be possible for me to be present, and I am very much obliged to you and the other officers of the League for the courtesy and compliment of the invitation." Faced with pressing foreign policy issues of neutrality both with Germany and the Allies, Wilson decided that he would assert his leadership on foreign policy with an embrace of the idea of an association of nations to preserve the peace against future wars.[45]

This turn of events made the weekend of 26–27 May a very gratifying one for William Howard Taft. During the afternoon of Friday, 26 May, he attended a White House tea party where, according to one newspaper account, his presence created a "Mild Furore." After greeting President and Mrs. Wilson, he moved through the guests where he was "seized upon by a score of folks eager to welcome him in the circle with which he formerly was so prominently identified." Then it was back to the first conference of the league, an event that attracted so many participants that it had to be moved from the New Willard Hotel to the Belasco Theater to accommodate the crowd. A local newspaper called it "the largest and most distinguished gathering of a voluntary character that ever assembled in this city."[46]

Wilson gave one of the most important speeches of his presidency on this occasion. He did not speak to the program of the league itself. Instead, he set forth his own vision of the kind of international organization he thought should exist after the current war came to a close. The listeners were enthralled, and a sense of common purpose blossomed in the drama of the moment. The nation's interest, Wilson concluded, is in "an universal association of the nations" to maintain freedom of the seas and to prevent future wars. The United States was willing "to become a partner in any feasible association of nations formed in order to realize these objects and make them secure against violation."[47]

The immediate reaction in the Belasco Theater and the nation was positive to both Wilson's speech and the work of the league itself in organizing the conference. Senator Henry Cabot Lodge, who spoke after Wilson, seemed to endorse as well the principles of some kind of association of nations. It would soon become apparent, however, that the senator's true attitude was less positive. For Taft, writing the next day to someone who could not attend, the news was all good. "We had a great meeting," he reported. They had "raised $375,000 to spread the propaganda of the League" and hoped to reach $500,000 "in bringing this matter to the attention of the American people. The accession of the President and Senator Lodge to the ranks of those who support our principles is of the highest importance."[48]

In his understandable zeal to have the president lend his approval to the work of the league, Taft failed to see that the identification with Wilson would have partisan consequences that would limit the future effectiveness of the peace group as a lobbying force. The main thrust of the league from the outset had been a conservative one that stressed legal remedies for international disputes. While there were Democrats among its membership, the majority of founders of the league were Republicans. There was thus an underlying tension between the league and the White House. With a bitter presidential campaign ahead, Republicans wanted Wilson's defeat by any means at their command. Providing support for his foreign policy goals was sure to irritate the GOP base.

The more that Wilson had, as one historian has put it, "secured for himself the leadership of the American peace movement," the more complex Taft's situation would become.[49] He wanted to see Wilson out of office, both because he disliked the Democrat's policies but also because only a Republican president could name him to the Supreme Court. Within a few weeks of the speech in late May, Taft would be signaling his willingness to mend fences with Roosevelt in the interest of a Republican election triumph in the autumn. His criticisms of Wilson in public would be sharp and intense. Working with Wilson in the common cause of ending the war and securing the peace and at the same time assailing him as incompetent and not deserving of a second term would test Taft's political skills through the rest of 1916. They would also limit his options in negotiating with the administration once Wilson had been returned to office.

4

THE ELECTION OF 1916 AND AMERICAN ENTRY INTO THE WAR

William Howard Taft had two goals for the 1916 election. Woodrow Wilson had to be defeated and Theodore Roosevelt could not be the Republican presidential nominee. Since he was convinced that selecting Roosevelt would doom the Republican cause and guarantee the re-election of the president, he could pursue both aims with equal intensity. He was to achieve one and fall short in the other, much to his regret. Wilson's victory over Charles Evans Hughes seemed to make any prospect of a Taft appointment to the Supreme Court even more remote than it had been after 1912.

In Wilson's first term, Taft had mustered some grudging respect for the incumbent as a political operator, even when he differed with the administration's progressive agenda. After witnessing Wilson's course in the Philippines, his handling of domestic issues, and above all his nomination of Brandeis, Taft had acquired a bitter taste about Wilson the man and chief executive. "I confess that my opinion of the President is distinctly lowered by his nomination of Brandeis," he told a reporter in March 1916. Taft recognized, however, that with war orders bringing renewed economic prosperity, Republicans would not have an easy time unseating the incumbent.[1]

In the wake of their 1912 debacle and then the eruption of war in Europe, the Republicans faced a complex set of problems as they looked toward a potential nominee. It was more than a matter of bringing the former Progressives back into the fold, a process that had shown some success during the 1914 elections. Neutrality and the question of military preparedness produced divisive strains within the Grand Old Party (GOP) coalition. Eastern Republicans such as Elihu Root were disposed to support intervention on the side of the Allies, or at least a more aggressive assertion of American rights toward Germany and in revolutionary Mexico.

In the center of the nation, progressive Republicans wanted to avoid the risk of war, and thus they opposed a more aggressive foreign policy. Among German-Americans, who provided a large share of Republican votes in the Midwest, the pro-Allied views of Root and the even more strident language of Theodore Roosevelt against Berlin evoked intense unhappiness. The Republicans sought a presidential candidate who could please all the factions within the party. He would have to be conservative enough to placate the right wing and progressive in ways that pleased reformers on domestic issues. In foreign policy, he would have to be firm enough on neutral rights to please party members in the East and yet not so warlike so that he alienated German-Americans and advocates of peace. The party needed a savior who could harmonize these diverse elements.

The potential Republican field seemed, with one exception, to be rather drab. From Taft's home state of Ohio, the names of Myron Herrick, a former governor, and Theodore E. Burton, a former senator, aroused little excitement. Robert M. La Follette had his own state of Wisconsin, friends in North Dakota, and little enthusiasm anywhere else. Albert B. Cummins of Iowa, once a progressive but now becoming ever more conservative, had backers in the Midwest, but few Republicans regarded him as a serious choice. Elihu Root, who was Taft's favorite, was nearing seventy, carried the baggage of having blocked Roosevelt at the 1912 convention, and drew anger from peace advocates for his interventionist position.

That left two genuine alternatives, Theodore Roosevelt and Charles Evans Hughes. In Taft's mind, the selection of his bitterest political enemy would have been an intolerable result. Fortunately for his peace of mind, the prospect of a Roosevelt nomination in 1916 did not thrill most Republicans either. There remained the residual anger of Roosevelt's bolt in 1912, which most Republicans believed had cost the party the White House. In addition,

Roosevelt's positions on the war, neutrality, and President Wilson seemed so extreme that his selection would almost guarantee another defeat in 1916.

Roosevelt had adopted such an anti-Wilson, pro-Allied stance in his public rhetoric that entry into the war upon his election as president seemed a likely result. He said in March 1916 that his nomination would be possible only if "the country has in its mood something of the heroic." He also made clear his distaste for German-Americans—or hyphenated Americans, as he labeled them—who were sympathetic to Berlin. Nominating Roosevelt would bring a renewal of the animosities of 1912, with divisions over neutrality added to the mixture. For an electorate eager to stay out of the European battles, Roosevelt had only limited appeal.[2]

Nonetheless, Roosevelt and his allies made several moves toward positioning himself in case the Republicans and the Progressive Party, whose remnants he still led, might find common cause behind his candidacy. Taft watched every flurry of Roosevelt sentiment with apprehension and political disgust. He was anxious that the party "should nominate a real Republican, and not be led astray into any foolish move like that of nominating Roosevelt, or anyone who was not a regular Republican in 1912." Still, he feared that "there is going to be a grand effort to nominate Roosevelt."[3]

The only logical alternative to the disaster of a Roosevelt nomination, in Taft's mind, would be the selection of what seemed the strongest Republican choice, Charles Evans Hughes. The Supreme Court justice seemed everyone's preferable selection in the very weak Republican field of 1916. Hughes had first probed corruption in the insurance industry before becoming governor of New York in 1907. He had been a strong executive until Taft elevated him to the high court in 1910. The jurist had rejected all offers to be a compromise candidate between Roosevelt and Taft in 1912. He thus had none of the political baggage of that Republican battle. Few Republicans noted that it had been a decade since Hughes had fought a contested election in 1906, when he ran against William Randolph Hearst for the governorship of New York.

Taft had great respect for Hughes as a judicial thinker. When

Charles Evans Hughes. Taft hoped that a victory for Charles Evans Hughes in 1916 might restore the Republicans to power and revive his own Supreme Court hopes. The Republican defeat was very disappointing as a result. (Library of Congress LC-DIG-hec-02423)

Hughes crafted the decision in a set of railroad cases in 1913, Taft had written to thank him, from the perspective of

"a struggling teacher of Constitutional law for the benefit you have conferred on my newest profession by your opinion in the Minnesota Rate cases and especially part of it in which you review the cases and their purport which make the line of distinction between that branch of interstate commerce which calls for uniform treatment and which the states must not touch and the remainder which permits of local treatment until Congress speaks."[4]

Their mutual respect as lawyers drew Hughes and Taft together.

Taft thus looked forward to a Hughes candidacy with a great deal of anticipation. He understood the misgivings that many Republican politicians felt about the reserved, bearded jurist. As governor of New York, Hughes had alienated many of the professionals with his lofty and often condescending manner. Theodore Roosevelt had to coerce many party members in the Empire State into supporting Hughes for re-election in 1908. As Taft reported in March 1916, "the politicians generally—the regulars—don't care for Hughes because they are afraid he will not have sufficient sense of party obligation. I think in this respect they are mistaken. I think he has learned a good deal since he was Governor of New York, and I think he will have more sense and a greater breadth of view."[5]

As momentum for Hughes accelerated, Taft and other politicians recalled how one of his speeches as a surrogate for Taft in 1908—attacking William Jennings Bryan—had done so much damage to the Democratic nominee in that year. If Hughes could do to Woodrow Wilson what he had done to Bryan eight years earlier, then the Republicans could have a good chance to regain the White House. For Taft the Hughes candidacy glimmered as his best option to bring the Republicans back into power and, at the same time, dash any chance of a Roosevelt rebound. Like many Republicans in 1916, Taft saw only the positive side of a Hughes nomination as the convention approached.

The former president thus blinked away some cautionary signs about the supreme court justice as presidential candidate. Hughes had never been truly tested in national politics. He had first been elected in New York in 1906 against William Randolph Hearst, the maverick and, at that time, radical newspaper publisher. Hearst made it a tough race, but with the support of then President Roosevelt and Elihu Root, Hughes had been pulled through to victory. In 1908 Governor Hughes faced opposition for renomination that Roosevelt quelled in the interest of a Taft victory. Taft put Hughes on the Supreme Court in 1910, and the new justice had been able to remain silent on the major political issues for the next six years.

Nonetheless, Taft was a significant encouraging element in a potential Hughes candidacy. He wrote to the justice to press upon him the necessity of defeating Wilson as a compelling reason to leave the court. He encouraged Hughes to make an exception to the wise precept that sitting justices should remain aloof from politics. Gradually the resolve that Hughes had shown not to abandon his seat gave way to the importunities of the Republicans that only he could save the nation from what Taft called "the organized incapacity of the country," i.e., Wilson and the Democrats.[6]

Taft got his wish in early June 1916 when the Republicans met in Chicago. The residue of the Progressive Party also assembled nearby in the city. The GOP named Hughes on the third ballot and proposed a platform with some modest nods in the direction of progressive reform. In the meantime, Roosevelt abandoned what remained of his third party and declared that he would support Hughes because of the imperative to beat Wilson. Hughes resigned from the court and prepared to launch what Republicans hoped and expected would be a vigorous campaign against Wilson. Taft met with the nominee at the end of June and told reporters, "I was very anxious to see Governor Hughes, and will do all I can to see him elected."[7]

One key to Republican victory in the minds of the Hughes managers was to heal the rift of 1912 between Taft and Roosevelt. If the two one-time friends and now bitter enemies could arrange a public reconciliation, the resulting boost for the Hughes ticket might

Taft and the League to Enforce Peace. The league was Taft's favorite foreign policy cause during American neutrality as well as when war came in 1917. He is shown here with other members of the group. (Library of Congress LC-DIG-hec-03413)

prove decisive. With the support of Taft already in hand, Hughes moved on 28 June to meet with Roosevelt and nail down his formal support. Their meeting was friendly and positive, but reporters noted that no disclosure "about the possibility of a reconciliation between Mr. Taft and Colonel Roosevelt was given out."[8]

In their meeting on 30 June, Hughes asked Taft if he would end his feud with Roosevelt. According to reporters with information from the campaign, Taft agreed "to do everything in his power—even to forget his differences with the Colonel—in order to elect Mr. Hughes." Hughes was reported to be working hard to that end in the faith that "public knowledge of such a reunion would be a most helpful thing in the campaign to elect him as president."[9]

The events that followed took on something of a comic opera quality as the Hughes campaign, which encountered general organizational difficulty from the beginning, sought to get Taft and

Roosevelt together in some friendly public setting. Roosevelt remained very cool to the idea of a reunion that might involve more than a formal handshake with his adversary on behalf of Hughes. In mid-September, the *New York Times* said, "It can be stated on the highest authority that the differences between the one-time friends have not been patched up to such an extent, and though each will make several speeches, they will be delivered from widely separated platforms."[10]

Taft told his brother Horace in mid-September that he had informed Elihu Root and the Hughes campaign "that I was not anxious to meet Roosevelt any more than he was anxious to meet me, but that we were both sincerely interested in electing Hughes, and that if our coming together would help in that direction, I was entirely willing." The outcome was an announcement from the Hughes campaign and gleeful Republicans that on 3 October 1916 the two men would encounter each other at the Union League Club in New York City. With Hughes in attendance, "the meeting of the two ex-presidents is expected to mark the climax of the festivities arranged as a triumphant token of a reunited party."[11]

Taft understood that he would be leaving the initiative to Roosevelt in the proposed meeting: "His influence with the reporters is such that he always secures the advantage." Roosevelt was not pleased with the arrangements of the Hughes campaign to play up the "reunion." According to reporters, he had told friends, "I will make no advance to shake hands with Mr. Taft. I will be in the receiving line and I will shake hands with Mr. Taft only in the same manner that I did at Professor Lounsbury's funeral in New Haven. I would do the same thing with Mr. Barnes, or with Mr. Root, if they were in line. This attempt to make it a reconciliation between myself and Mr. Taft is all wrong." Of course, there was no other rationale for the meeting, but Roosevelt, who could be as good a "hater" as Taft, wanted to preserve the facade that he was not there simply to be seen shaking hands with Taft. When the prospect arose of a campaign button with pictures of Roosevelt, Taft, and Hughes, Roosevelt called such a scheme "outrageous. It is an attempt to becloud the issues."[12]

The editorial writers of the *New York Times* labeled Roosevelt an "implacable Indian, he will not pretend to forgive. The bubble of harmony is dissolved." When the great moment came, a formal handshake was all that occurred. Republicans put out what a later generation would call "spin" to enhance the moment when the two men said at most a chilly hello. Taft's friends quoted their principal as saying, "We shook hands as any gentlemen might do and there was not a word said." Roosevelt then gave a speech attacking Wilson with his usual stridency. Taft, for his part, told the audience "that this election is the most important election that we have had in this country since the war."[13]

Republican papers said that the gathering had exceeded "all hopes of promoters." More objective observers found the moment a political failure. It became apparent that the two men had not said a solitary word to each other. A friend of Taft's reported that Union League club members had told him "that you conducted yourself as you always do—most creditably—last night in a trying situation and that the other man, as usual, conducted himself in the opposite way." In the end, the celebrated handshake did not affect the race much either way. The Hughes campaign had gotten off to a difficult start and the nominee had more problems than a made-for-cameras reconciliation between Roosevelt and Taft could have remedied.[14]

One reason that the Taft-Roosevelt meeting seemed so urgent stemmed from the Republican disappointment in Hughes as a presidential contender. Far from galvanizing the rank and file of his party and making a positive case against Wilson, the former jurist had proved a disappointing speaker who failed to inspire the friendly crowds he attracted. The acceptance speech had fallen flat, and Hughes could not frame a coherent critique of Wilson's policies. A tour of the west did not go well, and a cynical reporter told Roosevelt, "Hughes is dropping icicles from his beard all over the west and will return to New York clean shaven."[15]

Taft received similar intelligence from Gus Karger. "The Republican campaign keeps staggering on," he wrote on 14 September. "As yet Mr. Hughes has created no enthusiasm and his management remains execrable." Robert A. Taft reported in from Ohio on the troubles that the Republicans faced in a state that Hughes had to carry to have a plausible chance of success. "Everybody seems to dislike Hughes without exactly knowing why and the knowledge that you were enthusiastic for him would help a lot," the younger Taft concluded. His father recognized the continuing defects in the Republican candidate. He commented later in the campaign that Hughes "has very little lightness, and his speeches are like legal arguments as if he were talking to a jury."[16]

The Republicans got an apparent lift in early September when Wilson and the Democratic Congress passed the Adamson Act to avert a nationwide railroad strike. The railroad unions received the eight-hour day they sought. For the GOP, this was evidence of Democratic deference to the unions, and it enabled Hughes and Taft to inveigh against "Wilson's complete subservience to labor leadership." In fact, the support that Wilson picked up from progressives over the issue offset Republican unhappiness.[17]

Still hopeful that Wilson would not prevail, but worried as the Hughes effort faltered, Taft resolved not to hold back anything to defeat the president and the Democrats. For the rest of the 1916 campaign, Taft took to the hustings to indict the Wilson record and make the case for Hughes. Two days after his meeting with Hughes and Roosevelt, he began his campaign tour in New Jersey with an attack on Wilson's handling of labor unions and the Adamson Act. "Unwise subserviency to the demands of the leaders of organized labor finds its crowning instance in Mr. Wilson's dealing with the threatened strike of the railroad orders." He reviewed the Wilson performance on the civil service and in Mexico and renewed his complaint that the incumbent was a chronic opportunist. The president, Taft told his audience, "has few, if any, opinions on the issues of the day which exigency in the field of politics may not induce him to give up."[18]

His most elaborate anti-Wilson statement came in a lengthy article that he prepared for the *Yale Review* under the title of "The Democratic Record." In the pages of this extensive critique of Wilson and his policies, Taft elaborated on the charges he was making about the president on the campaign trail. He had no patience for the "suggestion that criticism of the foreign policy of the administration is unpatriotic." Taft had withheld comments about the White House and its performance and had restrained "criticism of his course which would weaken his weight with our nations by making it appear that our people were divided in their views of our rights or their determination to maintain them." In an election year, however, "it is absurd to say that when the question is whether we shall continue the President as the guide of our international affairs, we may not properly discuss and criticize in all its details his conduct of our foreign relations."[19]

With that explanatory prelude out of the way, Taft then launched into an all-out demolition of Wilson's presidential performance. Only in the case of the Federal Reserve Act had Wilson done something constructive, and even that achievement, in Taft's mind, owed much to the prior work of Senator Nelson Aldrich and the Republicans. On the other controversial foreign policy subjects, Wilson either had fallen short, such as in the case of the Philippines or Mexico, or had changed his views since entering politics. Taft came down with special force against the president's course in the railroad strike and the Adamson Act, where Wilson had deferred to organized labor. "The whole episode is one of the most humiliating in the nation's history and is fraught with far-reaching evil consequences."[20]

The contrast between Wilson and Hughes, for Taft, was striking. Where Wilson bent to the political winds, Hughes "is a man whose convictions have always been the guide of his action." To the proposition that there were scant differences between the two candidates and therefore Wilson's experience should carry the day, Taft concluded that it "would be difficult to find among the public men of the country a man who is less like Mr. Wilson than Mr. Hughes."[21]

As October progressed and election day neared, Taft remained hopeful of a Hughes victory, but there continued to be worrying signs. His son Robert renewed his warnings that Hughes might lose Ohio. Gus Karger reported that Hughes had become a better campaigner but at Republican headquarters he found "dissatisfaction with many things and many jealousies and heartburnings." Roosevelt's warlike speeches were alienating the German-American vote and emphasizing the power of the Democratic slogan about Wilson, "He Kept Us Out of War." In a letter to Mabel Boardman, Taft conceded that "the campaign management is very poor, but I am hopeful that the elements of the situation, making Hughes's election probable will overcome the defects of management."[22]

At the end of the campaign, Taft sought to deliver an address to a crowd at a munitions factory in New Haven. The audience was unfriendly, and he had just started to speak when the booing began. He pressed on for a few minutes and was "jeered and hooted to such an extent that he was obliged to abandon his speech." Taft commented to reporters, "I have no complaint to make. Such demonstrations, I am convinced, make votes for the Republican Party."[23]

When the election occurred, early signs indicated a Hughes victory in the east. As the returns continued, however, Wilson's strength in the west, and his success in California, enabled the Democrat to win one of the closest elections in the nation's history. He secured 277 electoral votes to 254 for Hughes, and thus secured a second term. Taft was crushed. "The election was a great disappointment to me, although for two weeks I have been in a state of fear that that was about to occur which did occur." Taft placed some of the blame on "the emotional nature of women just endowed with the right to vote" and the peace vote in the west. The inept management of the Hughes campaign irked him as well. As a British observer remarked at the time, "No American campaign that I have seen has been worse managed than the Republican one."[24]

The real drawback to the Hughes campaign for Taft was the undue emphasis it had placed on obtaining the support of Theodore Roosevelt. Propitiating Roosevelt made political sense, but the Hughes managers "over did it. It was a mistake to have Roosevelt make those bitter speeches which he made late in the campaign. They only served to strengthen the slogan: 'He kept us out of war.' by lending support to Wilson's statement that if Hughes were elected he would involve us in war."[25] Once again, Roosevelt's political ambitions had thwarted Republican hopes, with the result that Taft's hopes for a Supreme Court appointment receded.

He consoled himself with the rationalization that even if Hughes had won and named him to the court, the Senate would not have confirmed his nomination. "But certainly it is out of the question now, and I am entirely reconciled pursuing the even temper of my way as I am. I find myself swamped with work, and my great trouble," he informed Mabel Boardman, "is that I am not able to do as thorough work as I would like to do."[26]

As exciting as the 1916 election had been for Taft, the months that followed proved even more tumultuous as the United States moved from peace to involvement in World War I. President Wilson sought to be a mediator in the world conflict and invited the belligerents to state their war aims, with the goal of bringing the parties to a peace conference. When his initiative went nowhere, the president articulated his vision of a peace settlement in his "Peace Without Victory" address to Congress on 22 January 1917. Nine days later, the Germans handed the White House an ultimatum that announced that a return of unrestricted submarine warfare would begin the next day. On February 3, Wilson declared that the United States had broken diplomatic relations with the German Empire.

These months became a time of intense vicarious involvement in the foreign policy process for Taft. He and the League to Enforce Peace saw President Wilson adopting positions about the need for international organization that gave credence to their cause. In his own public appearances, Taft seconded what the president had said about America's new role in the world. At the National Press Club on 19 January 1917, he told the reporters gathered there that "we have got to go all in" for world affairs and that "it is to our great interest to see to it that we exercise every influence that we can to prevent another world war."[27]

Three days later Wilson appeared before Congress to say that only a "peace without victory" that treated all the belligerents fairly would prevent another world conflict. The president asserted that there would have to be a force established to preserve any peace settlement "so much greater than the force of any nation now engaged or any alliance hitherto formed." Only "the organized major force of mankind" could perform that function. Speaking in Bangor, Maine, to the Bangor Theological Seminary, Taft called Wilson's address "an epoch in our foreign policy. His advocacy of our participation in the world league is the most powerful aid to its formation."[28]

In private, however, Taft had reservations about how the president had framed his endorsement of the principles of the league. He had done so, Taft told his old friend and former Massachusetts senator, Winthrop Murray Crane, "in such a way as to embarrass me, because I don't agree with much of what he says in respect to the kind of peace that ought to be achieved." The former president did not like the idea of a resolution of the war "without the victory of the Allies." Taft could not say that in public because what Wilson had done "is an agitation for the League and that is a good thing."[29]

Taft's public enthusiasm for Wilson's speech and his endorsement of a league of nations to maintain the peace posed a political problem for the former president that would plague him for the next four years. While there was initial enthusiasm for Wilson's "Peace Without Victory" address, it did not take long before Senate Republicans expressed criticisms of the lofty concept that the president was advancing. Theodore Roosevelt had already assailed Taft and the League to Enforce Peace as "silly" and guilty of "milk and water" policies. Taft replied that "it would have added to the usefulness of his criticism if he had read carefully the proposals of the league."[30]

Roosevelt, Senator William E. Borah of Idaho, and other Republicans launched waves of criticism at Wilson's speech soon after it was delivered. They also attacked the League to Enforce Peace, which Lodge said did not "any longer" represent "my opinion." That result left Taft in a dilemma that would affect his actions over the next three years. If he wanted to achieve some sort of international body to preserve world peace, he could not get too far away from Wilson, the only man in the United States who could lead the nation into such an organization. Yet the more that Taft identified himself with the president's policies, the more problems he faced with his skeptical Republican colleagues. They believed that Wilson had lied his way to re-election and was undeserving of bipartisan political assistance. To retain any influence with his party in the event of a Republican electoral victory in 1918 and 1920, Taft had to find a middle ground on the peace question.[31]

As the international situation with Germany deteriorated in February and March of 1917, Taft joined those who were urging a tough response to the unrestricted submarine warfare that Berlin had declared. "We are now in a crisis," he proclaimed on 5 February in a speech to a League to Enforce Peace chapter in Brooklyn, New York. "We are going to rally behind the President." The next day, he reiterated: "How can we proceed on the doctrines of isolation from European quarrels sitting back in a rocking chair and saying we don't care what happens. Even from a selfish standpoint it is unwise." Several weeks later, he went so far as to say: "If the life of my son were sacrificed in a war between Austria and Serbia, in which we had no concern, through the entry of the United States into that war to localize its fire and prevent its involving the entire world, the sacrifice would be worthwhile."[32] In March he announced that he would conduct a "Paul Revere" tour to rouse support for a policy of preparedness in the face of the impending German threat.[33]

In early February, Taft came out in support of a draft to raise the army needed to fight the impending war and maintain the peace. By endorsing conscription and playing down a reliance on volunteers, he was making a case against the raising of a volunteer division to fight overseas that Theodore Roosevelt had proposed to form and lead. Taft worried about "such a mushroom growth of volunteer regiments as we had in the Spanish War." The Wilson administration had not yet resolved the question of how an army would be raised, but Secretary of War Newton D. Baker appreciated the support Taft had accorded to the White House in the looming battle with Roosevelt.[34]

When war came to the United States in April 1917, Taft gave public support to the administration in the initial stages of belligerency.

However, he continued his skepticism over Roosevelt's effort to take an advance guard of American forces to France. Taft shared the view of the White House that the war effort required a more professional approach to assembling an army than Roosevelt realized. "It would," he wrote James Bryce in England, "involve great risk to entrust 25,000 men to a commander so lacking in real military experience and so utterly insubordinate in his nature."[35]

Having volunteered his son in a rhetorical flourish before the war, Taft saw the thought become a reality once the United States was a belligerent power. His oldest son, Robert A. Taft, had bad eyesight and could not pass the physical requirements for enlistment. Instead, he joined Herbert Hoover in the United States Food Administration, and in time followed Hoover to Europe as part of the peace delegation to Paris. The former president's youngest child, Charles P. Taft, enlisted in the artillery at the age of nineteen and became engaged, all within a short span of time. Meanwhile, Taft's daughter Helen was named dean of the faculty at Bryn Mawr College outside Philadelphia at the young age of twenty-six.[36]

Taft fretted about his youngest boy who, at nineteen, seemed both too young to be off to war and to be engaged to be married and then to be wed even before his unit was sent to France. After Charles enlisted, his father told him that "it is a great comfort to me that you are a member of the church, that you don't smoke, and that you don't drink, and that you have those high ideals that enable you to elevate the people about you rather than to yield to their leveling or lowering tendency." Since Charles had gone to Yale, he could use his "influence to keep the Yale boys straight, and if you do so with them, they will be able to influence the rest." When Charles went to France, Will Taft wrote to a Cincinnati friend, Mrs. Lucien Wulsin, who lived in Paris so that his son could have "home friends in Paris."[37]

For his own part, William Howard Taft was in constant demand for speeches about the League to Enforce Peace and the shape of the world once the fighting ended. During much of 1917, however, his time was taken up with his renewed activity on behalf of the American Red Cross. The organization had been reshaped since

Taft's decision that Mabel Boardman's leadership had to give way to more masculine direction. She had been eased out of any control over the operation of the Red Cross in favor of a man named Eliot Wadsworth. He in turn had shut her out of the daily workings of the Red Cross, and she had to content herself with scraps of her former influence. As Taft told his brother Horace in September 1916, "I had a good deal of trouble in arranging the transfer of power in the Red Cross from her to Eliot Wadsworth, who is now the Vice Chairman. She found it difficult not to interfere."[38]

That the change left hard feelings was evident from Taft's efforts to reassure her that she would in time adjust to the loss of status and influence. "I know something of a taking away of responsibility and of occupation of one's hours, and I know how you feel. However, you will get used to it and you will open lines of activity that will interest you greatly." Of course, Taft had lost his authority as a result of a national election and a democratic process. Boardman had been replaced in an internal coup engineered by someone she regarded as a very close friend.[39]

In the spring of 1917, once the United States was in the war, both the president and the leadership of the Red Cross saw extensive fund-raising as the key for the organization to carry out its greatly expanded duties. As the nation raised a huge conscription army, the role of the Red Cross would be not only to aid and assist the draftees as they transitioned to their assigned fighting fronts, but also to help sustain their families. Elihu Root questioned whether such activities were justified under the Geneva Convention and the Red Cross charter. Taft thought that Root's reservations were "an absurdly fine point not to be sustained by anything in the Convention or the law or the regulations."[40] In the end, of course, Taft's view prevailed.

Taft met with Woodrow Wilson at the White House on 28 April 1917. The former president told reporters that "we must get down to a war basis. Many things which are proper in peace time are not efficient with the nation at war. The Red Cross is preparing to do its part in the war." When, however, Taft sought to retire as the chair of the Executive Committee of the Red Cross, President

Wilson asked him to "reconsider your request to me and accede to the desire which we all entertain, and entertain most earnestly, that you should retain that position." Taft agreed and plunged into the campaign to accumulate $100 million for the Red Cross.[41] The president and Taft were at the dedication of the Red Cross building on 5 May 1917. The wife of a Texas House member said that they were on the stage "side by each" in what she called "altogether the glummest performance, not a ray of real feeling throughout."[42]

On the stump for the Red Cross, Taft warned his listeners that "upon America is to rest the terrible burdens to come." He found "the feeling among our American people is lax" and they did not recognize that France in particular would need extensive assistance. "We of this country must rehabilitate that country." Whether he was speaking for the Red Cross or the League to Enforce Peace, and he did both on some occasions, Taft stressed the need for national sacrifice. The United States was fighting the German people and the aggressive militarism that they supported. They were "a people obsessed with megalomania, and the only way we can win is by hitting the German people with a club."[43]

Throughout June 1917, Taft gave as many as eight speeches for the Red Cross campaign and more for the Young Men's Christian Association (YMCA) as well: "I received no compensation for these addresses." He also donated $3,000 himself to the $100 million campaign. So when the YMCA did not send his compensation of $300 for a speech in New London, he asked them where the money was. By the time Taft reached Murray Bay for the summer of 1917, he had expended a prodigious amount of his time and energy for the Red Cross, the Liberty Loan campaign, the YMCA, and the League to Enforce Peace. There were even reports that Taft would be summoned to manage the raising of the army through the draft, but those revelations had no basis in fact.[44]

One reform associated with the war did not attract Taft's support. Though he did not drink alcohol himself at all, he had never been an admirer of prohibition. He regarded it as "an outrage that prohibition cranks who are looking to secure prohibition in peace time should use the present situation to attempt to force prohibition on the country. The arbitrary methods of war are bad enough in themselves, but to have them enlarged and emphasized to gratify the theories of extremists in normal government is most aggravating and wasteful."[45]

During his Canadian vacation, the public sought Taft's opinions on the events associated with the war and the changes in American society. About the race riot in East St. Louis that erupted during the summer, when whites rioted against blacks, Taft had nothing but scorn for the failure of local authorities to protect African Americans. Blacks, he wrote, "had the constitutional right to enjoy the same protection extended by Illinois to all of its laboring men and women, white or black." The police in East St. Louis and the Illinois militia had shown "weakness, political cowardice, and utter inefficiency" in their handling of the violence.[46]

The tensions of the war also brought at least one long-standing friendship to a temporary end. Jacob G. Schmidlapp, a prominent Cincinnati banker and leader in that city's German American community, wrote Taft defending the German position in the war. After an exchange of letters in which their disagreement proved unbridgeable, Taft said, "I don't think it wise to continue our correspondence." Taft told his old friend that "we are in a life and death struggle for our liberty and that of the world, and those who are not for us are against us." Schmidlapp, Taft concluded, did not "seem to appreciate the spirit of individual liberty which lies at the basis of our government." The two men resumed their correspondence in time, but for the moment Taft had little patience with friends who did not share his views on the war.[47]

By early August, Taft had left Murray Bay to go back on the road for the war effort. At Clay Center, Kansas, his overexertions produced a medical setback. He had a stomach attack that put him in the hospital for several days. President Wilson sent him a telegram of concern, to which Taft replied, "I am better and hope to be out in a few days." The doctors told the press that "the speaking trip which Mr. Taft is now on has been too much for him." By the middle of the month, the patient was recovering, and he returned to Murray Bay for the rest of the month.[48]

Even with his improved physical condition and postpresidential weight loss, Taft knew that he could not continue the intense pace of cross-country lecturing he had followed since 1913. He turned sixty in mid-September and a slower pace of work seemed imperative, yet he needed the money that he earned from lecturing. A solution presented itself after he repelled a public challenge to his position on prosecuting the war against Germany.

At the end of September, Taft went to Montreal for a meeting of the Unitarian Conference, where policy for the church would be set. Taft served as president of the gathering, and on 26 September he called on the Reverend John Haynes Holmes of New York City to present a report on the church's attitude toward the European conflict. A pacifist, Holmes had framed a document that did not come out for an Allied victory. Instead, "he had tried to state the varying views of the Unitarian body and then find some common ground on which they could all unite for the bringing about of the kingdom of God."[49]

As Taft sat on the stage and listened to Holmes, he bridled when the minister said that the war was "an ugly piece of business that must be done." One reporter noted that "as the reading progressed, the ex-President's face grew redder, and by the time the last phrase was out his cheeks were fiery." Taft asked permission to leave the chair, address the audience, and offer a resolution: "As a literary expression, this report is beautiful, but as an expression, at this time, of the opinion of this body of churchmen, it is an insidious document." To a now cheering assembly, Taft asked, "Are we in favor of winning the war or are we not? That is the question." The crowd shouted back its agreement.[50]

Taft then proposed a resolution that stated: "The opinion of this Unitarian conference that this war must be carried to a successful issue to stamp out militarism in this world." The language added support of "the measures of President Wilson and Congress, restrictive though they may be." Speaking for his resolution, Taft said, "I am not a pacifist. This is a righteous war, and when you fight a righteous war you must win." The resolution passed by a vote of 236 to 6. The Unitarians ousted clergy who did not endorse the war, and Holmes and his members left the church. Years after the war, the Unitarians recanted these actions.[51] For the moment, however, Taft had identified his church with the passions of the war effort.

Taft enjoyed a public triumph at Montreal and he also made a commitment to become a regular newspaper columnist. Cyrus H. K. Curtis, owner of the Philadelphia *Public Ledger*, asked the former president for a meeting in New Haven a few days after the conference. There the publisher invited Taft to become a contributing editor for the newspaper. He would be paid $10,000 per year and would write a column each week on a subject of his own choosing. The arrangement required some adjustment on Taft's part at first, but he soon got into the rhythm of column-writing. Skeptical of his talent as a newspaper writer, he found that he enjoyed the ability to command public attention.[52]

The columns gave Taft a powerful opportunity to influence public opinion. He did not achieve the impact of Theodore Roosevelt's similar work for the *Kansas City Star* during 1918, but Taft continued for two and a half years after Roosevelt's death in January 1919. His contributions received ample press coverage and were particularly important during the battle over the League of Nations in 1919 and 1920. Never a pithy pundit, his columns often resembled legal briefs more than crisp statements of opinion. The management of the newspaper enjoyed the prestige that his presence conveyed. Major newspapers reprinted what the former president had said, and a number of his commentaries made news.

As it developed, during 1918 Taft would go to work with the National War Labor Board in Washington in a manner that both interrupted his teaching at Yale and gave him a different role in the war. The writing for the *Public Ledger* thus proved a reliable source of funds and a congenial way to keep his thoughts relevant in the public arena.

The larger problem for Taft in 1918 was the difficult relationship he had with President Wilson as well as with his own party. Committed to the agenda of the League to Enforce Peace, he wanted to see an international organization come out of the war with the judicial machinery to prevent another world conflict. The president, however, wanted to retain the power to shape the peace settlement on his own without interference, especially from the conservatives who, in Wilson's mind, dominated the league. For their part, Republicans such as Elihu Root, Henry Cabot Lodge, and Theodore Roosevelt believed that Taft should never have aligned himself with the White House in any way. Balancing these two pressures while still achieving his goals for a world organization would be Taft's main problem throughout 1918.

5

FROM THE FOURTEEN POINTS TO THE 1918 ELECTION

During 1918, William Howard Taft cooperated with the Wilson administration by serving as one of the cochairs of the National War Labor Board, the purpose of which was to preserve industrial peace for the war effort. The former president toured army camps to inspire troops with the reasons they were fighting. Despite this demonstration of domestic unity with the administration and the war effort, the year further emphasized the differences between Woodrow Wilson and Taft over the issue of world organization and the preservation of peace once the fighting ended. Serious fissures developed as Taft pressed for details and the president resisted spelling out his vision of a league of nations.

Taft's reconciliation with Theodore Roosevelt added to the complexity. As the two onetime friends renewed their friendship over their common dislike of Wilson and the Democrats, the strains between Taft and the White House intensified. The partisanship that Roosevelt displayed in the 1918 congressional contest moved Taft back toward his party. In the process, Wilson became convinced that Taft could not be trusted as a reliable ally. This outcome would be an element in Wilson's ultimate failure to achieve the League of Nations in 1919–1920.

Throughout the autumn of 1917, in his speeches and then in his column, Taft insisted that Germany must be conquered to achieve any kind of lasting peaceful world. "Our object is to inflict such a defeat on Germany that she will give up purpose of future conquest."

To that end, "an absolute necessity" existed "for ending the military domination of Germany if we are to have peace in the world," he told a Brooklyn audience on 9 January 1918. If Americans committed open treason, Taft said a month later, they should receive "the short shrift of the firing squad" against "a blank wall at sunrise." He also denounced "whisperers who are covertly sowing sedition and pro-German propaganda."[1]

The leaders of the Young Men's Christian Association (YMCA), fearful that the young men drafted into the war effort did not know what they were fighting for, asked Taft to make a tour of army camps to describe the rationale for the struggle against Germany. The association posed a question to him in July 1917, "whether an American victory for the Allies is worth dying for." Taft responded: "We are in the war, first of all, to make the world a safer and better place to live in." During the remainder of the year and into 1918, he took the message to the training camps across the country on behalf of the YMCA's War Work Council. He disdained the idea of a negotiated settlement of the conflict. "Stamp on all proposals of peace as ill advised or seditious, and then time will make for our certain victory."[2]

Despite his age and other commitments to war work, Taft kept his wife current on his tour of army cantonments during February 1918. He addressed thousands of soldiers at each stop and told reporters that "the drafted men are already good soldiers and will make the best in the world." On the trip he watched with dismay as President Wilson consolidated his government to improve the nation's war effort. For Taft, these moves indicated Wilson's "lust for power, his impatience with any restriction by Congress and his calm self-confidence."[3]

Believing that the League to Enforce Peace was an important element in assisting the White House in pursuing the war, Taft and his associates wanted to have links with President Wilson to coordinate their appeal for an international organization with the government. Wilson distrusted Taft and the conservatives who formed much of the league's leadership. Moreover, the president did not want to spell out the details of any peace plan lest the political opposition pick the scheme apart. He thus regarded Taft with some suspicion. Wilson also was convinced that Taft's intellect was inferior to his own, a point he did not hide from the former president. For his part, Taft continued to believe that opportunism and partisanship were the president's dominant traits. "He has been on every side of every subject," Taft wrote a friend in Paris, "and he is a pacifist at heart."[4]

As a result of these temperamental divergences, the two men could at best achieve an uneasy cooperation. They met at the White House in mid-December 1917 to discuss the suggestion that Taft might go to England to explain American war aims to the people of this major ally of the United States. Upon their return, these informal emissaries could provide the American people with "a more accurate idea of the British people." Taft had been invited to participate. He came to the White House to ask the president if "his going would not seem unwise for any reason."[5]

A disapproving Wilson told Taft he should not undertake the mission. The United States and Great Britain had conflicting war aims as far as Wilson was concerned. The United States had unselfish aims while the British intentions "seemed of a less worthy character." Wilson advanced other considerations that led him to deprecate the possibility of Taft undertaking the mission to London. He concluded: "I think you ought not to go and the same applies to the other members of the party. I would like you to make my attitude on this question known to those having it in charge here."[6]

In the record of Taft's visit to the White House, there is a perceptible sense of abruptness and dislike from Wilson for the prospect of other individuals, especially Republicans, getting involved in the art of diplomacy and peacemaking in any fashion. Within a week Wilson would launch the process of establishing war aims that evolved into the Fourteen Points of January 1918. He did not appreciate Taft or anyone else participating in what he saw as a presidential prerogative in the realm of foreign policy. It did not occur to the aloof and self-sufficient Wilson that he might need reliable Republican help in the future. The question was whether Taft could provide bipartisanship or would revert to his life-long identification with the Grand Old Party when it came to an election campaign.

Taft and the leadership of the League to Enforce Peace wished to move ahead with their program for a post-war organization. They decided to hold another one of their periodic conventions to rouse enthusiasm for their ideas in May 1918. Working through a formidable structure of members and sub-leagues across the country, the league told the press that the gathering would instill enthusiasm for a victory that in turn would "create such effective guarantees that so far as is humanly possible that such a war shall not be gone through without gain, and that the world in the future shall be builded upon the foundations of justice, freedom, and democracy."[7]

President Wilson disliked the activism of the League to Enforce Peace in the winter of 1918. He feared that a meeting in Washington to discuss actual peace aims would hamper his freedom of action. In private he regarded Taft and the league as impractical and intrusive "butters-in" into the work of serious policymakers. The president sent one of his aides, Bainbridge Colby of the United States Shipping Board, to see Taft and tell him that the League to Enforce Peace should not hold its proposed convention. Colby relayed Wilson's apprehension that "at the Convention, details of the proposed League would be discussed by men of prominence, and that it would embarrass him in such communications as he might wish to make for peace when the time arrived."[8]

To bring the league under at least partial control, the president accepted, albeit with reluctance, the idea that he must see Taft and A. Lawrence Lowell, the president of Harvard University, to set them straight about what the league should and should not do. An elaborate process of invitation and consultation ensued. Out of these talks came a White House appointment for Taft and Lowell late in the afternoon of 28 March 1918. They met Wilson in the Green Room and settled down to business about the League to Enforce Peace, its plans, and Wilson's objections to any examination of peace details.

In the conversation, the president renewed his objections against any working out of specific peace programs at the meeting of the league. Once again he stressed that any "discussing and framing of such plans" could "embarrass him thereafter in dealing with the subject" of an international organization. Any kind of informal talks between British and American peace advocates or with their French counterparts should be out of bounds in Wilson's opinion. The three men discussed some general aspects of a peace settlement, the situation on the western front where the Germans had just launched a major offensive, and what the league members might say at their May gathering. As long as the League to Enforce Peace confined itself to exhortations about winning the war, Wilson had no objection.[9]

After he thought about the meeting and what the president had told them, Taft concluded that "Wilson does not favor our League to Enforce Peace." In private letters, the former president was scathing about the White House incumbent. On the issue of the shape of the postwar world, which so consumed Taft's thoughts throughout 1918, he was suspicious now of Wilson's good intentions. "I think if he could make peace, he would, without regard to his brave declarations that he would not deal with the Kaiser." The White House interview strengthened Taft's determination to push forward with the program of the league and to "fulfill an important function in winning this war by awakening among our people an irresistible crusading spirit."[10] In doing so, of course, Taft further demonstrated to the president that he could not be trusted to follow Wilson's lead in peacemaking.

The meeting of the League to Enforce Peace took place in Philadelphia on 16 May under the slogan, "Win the War for Permanent Peace." With more than 3500 delegates present, the organization laid out a program for swaying public opinion behind the league's program. As the main speaker, Taft preached the need for complete victory over Germany. "Let us have peace, but let us have war that we may have peace. To sound the trumpet for war to the end this convention was called." Only with the final defeat of Germany and the return of its conquests could the war come to a proper conclusion. "If the wrongs of the oppressed are not righted," Taft proclaimed, "the war will have been fought in vain."[11] None of what

Taft said persuaded Woodrow Wilson to consult the leaders of the league in the future. Nor did the president encourage them to interact with other supporters of an international league overseas. He urged the league not to "undertake to establish international connections" with foreign committees with the purpose of framing potential peace leagues."[12]

Taft and the other leaders of the league used the months between the convention and the elections in the autumn to build up the organizational structure of the group across the country. In September, Taft assured the Secretary of the Treasury William G. McAdoo that the league would support the bond-raising Fourth Liberty Loan for the war effort. "We are absolutely convinced," Taft wrote, "that victory is essential to the establishment of a permanent and effective League of Nations and [we] are making support of the war and opposition to a premature peace the most prominent features of our work."[13]

As an exponent of the war and an advocate of an international organization, Taft sought a larger role in policy-making, either as an informal adviser to Wilson or as a member of the administration in some serious capacity. Like many Republicans, he believed that the White House had kept the opposition party at arm's length. Wilson had thwarted Theodore Roosevelt's desire to send a division to France. Elihu Root's mission to Russia had failed. General Leonard Wood had been relegated to training duties in the United States. As Taft's friend, the former Senator Winthrop Murray Crane, observed in July 1918, "The Republicans have given President Wilson better and more loyal support than many of the Democrats" despite being kept on the sidelines.[14]

From Wilson's perspective, however, Crane, Taft, and other Republicans wanted the political equivalent of having everything both ways. While they desired a serious consultative role with the White House, they expected to make a partisan case against Wilson and the Democrats whenever they chose to do so. Democrats saw hypocrisy in the stated positions of the GOP.

While the White House did not give Taft a serious role within the administration, unrest and strikes among American workers did lead to his selection as a member of the National War Labor Board, created in the spring of 1918. In that capacity, the former president found himself much involved in the contested landscape of wartime labor relations. Chosen to represent the interests of the business community in the mediation and conciliation process that the board pursued throughout 1918, Taft proved to be less of a dogmatic conservative on labor issues than his business sponsors had expected.

By the end of 1917, informed observers in Washington knew that the labor policy of the Wilson administration needed an immediate overhaul. While both management and unions had pledged to support the war effort, the two sides also intended to pursue their own agendas as well. Labor strife mounted during the last eight months of the year. Inflation rose as producers hiked prices, unions struck for higher wages, and the war increased demand for all sorts of crops and goods. In a tighter labor market, workers staged walkouts to increase their income. Meanwhile, owners and operators sought to break unions and fire individuals who joined a labor organization. The resulting turmoil led to nearly three thousand strikes and over six million workdays lost to strikes.[15]

Within the Wilson administration, internal battles raged over labor policy. The president decided to leave the task of improving labor relations to the relevant cabinet official, Secretary of Labor William B. Wilson. Out of this process came Secretary Wilson's creation in late January 1918 of the National War Labor Board. It had five members from the management side, five members from labor. These representatives would then designate two members of the public to serve as cochairs of the body.

The union members selected a Kansas City lawyer, Frank P. Walsh, who was identified with support for labor causes. A few years earlier, Walsh had headed the Commission on Industrial Relations, which probed the situation of labor and management in American society. His inquiry had looked into the sprawling ranch of Charles P. Taft in South Texas. Walsh concluded that the giant agricultural enterprise exploited the workers who raised its crops. That charge led William Howard Taft to criticize Walsh as lacking

Frank P. Walsh. Though they were ideological opposites, Taft and Walsh cooperated well on the National War Labor Board in 1917–1918. (Library of Congress LC-USZ62-117861)

"judicial poise." This past history of a public dispute made it seem unlikely that the two men could collaborate on the new labor board.[16]

Such a consideration induced the management representatives to select Taft for their cochair of the board. For Taft, the assignment appealed to his sense of patriotism and public service. His record of ruling against labor unions as a federal judge in the 1890s made him seem a very safe choice to the business representatives on the proposed board. To some degree, they mistook Taft's judicial conservatism for a complete identification with the cause of business at large. However, Taft did not provide a simple yes vote for whatever the management position was in a particular labor dispute.

It turned out that Walsh and Taft, as fellow attorneys, found ways to cooperate during 1918. Walsh wielded his Irish charm to good effect, but Taft also operated in a collaborative spirit. As Taft told his brother Charles in August 1918, "in dealing with me behind closed doors, I have found him amenable. He is an Irishman, with all the camaraderie of an Irishman." The two men evolved a productive working relationship. Walsh's volatility often grated on the sensibilities of those he opposed. Taft acted as he had done under Theodore Roosevelt to soothe passions and develop a common position that the whole board could adopt. Taft functioned as a balance wheel for the board, much to the dismay of the management representatives on the panel.[17]

Taft came to the issue of labor relations without much practical experience about how working Americans lived. Though never rich in the opulent style of his brother Charles, he had always lived in a comfortable manner, in part thanks to his brother's regular generosity. With a summer home in Canada, secure government jobs from 1890 through 1913, and his position at Yale and lecturing income after the White House, Taft had never faced poverty or known of its challenges. He had not visited factories or sweatshops, seen agricultural workers in the fields close-up, or sent his young children out to the workplace to supplement the family income. He thus viewed unions from the perspective he had developed during the labor unrest of the 1890s, when trade-union leaders came to his courtroom to face criminal charges or confront an injunction. The education Taft would get in 1918 would not shake his basic conservatism, but it would underscore the limits of his knowledge about the full range of American economic life.

Accepting the government position in the spring of 1918 meant changes in Taft's lifestyle. He took a leave of absence from his teaching duties at Yale and rented an apartment in Washington for the duration of his labor assignment. "Nellie and I are getting ready to move our Lares and Penates to Washington," he wrote a friend in late May. "My labor in connection with the National War Labor Board is considerable," he added several months later. He took some time off at Murray Bay in the summer while a substitute member took his place on the board. "I have been working so hard this year that I need a vacation."[18]

The National War Labor Board had first to frame a set of principles that would guide its work. In two days of talks in late March, the twelve members came to a consensus that informed their work for the rest of the board's existence. Taft and Walsh created the board's mandate. As Taft told his wife, at a key moment the two men "compared notes, corrected language, modified details," and then had Taft's secretary "give us a fair copy of the whole." They then showed the document to the whole group "and by night when we met again we had agreed upon it."[19]

The board assumed that "there should be no strikes or lockouts during the war." The existing arrangements in factories and workplaces were to be left alone. Union shops would remain as they were; nonunion shops would not be altered either. The Taft-Walsh group also recognized in explicit terms the right of labor to organize. There followed eight principles that the board would follow in resolving disputes between labor and management. [20]

This statement of the principles gave organized labor more than many observers had predicted. Taft played an important part in the development of these concepts that would guide the proposed labor panel in its work. The guidelines for resolving disputes recognized the right to unionize and engage in collective bargaining while also extending the same right to employers to create their own groups within a workplace for the same purpose. Employers should not dismiss workers for joining a union and "the workers shall not coerce their fellows to join unions." In the case of women, when they did men's work they should "receive the same wages as do men." The final principle asserted that all workers deserved to receive "a living wage" sufficient to provide a degree of "health and reasonable comfort."[21]

Woodrow Wilson told Taft that the work of the panel would be "highly serviceable" to the nation as an example "of the spirit of cooperation and concession which is drawing our people together in this time of supreme crisis." The president moved the board from advisory to active status on 9 April 1918 with the creation of the National War Labor Board. In his fourteen months on the board, Taft surprised many observers—the business leaders who had recommended him in the first place, and probably himself—with his moderation and often pro-labor rulings in his role as joint chair. He and Walsh found themselves coming down together on the side of labor in key cases during the spring and autumn of 1918 until the war ended and Walsh resigned.[22]

In case after case, Taft's judicial temperament and instinct for compromise led him to frame a moderate response between capital and labor. His goal was to keep the wheels of industry turning and to avoid strikes as much as possible. When confronted with conditions in the plants and workplaces he visited in the course of engaging with specific companies and unions, Taft did display a willingness to expand the mandate of the board in certain cases. For example, he insisted that scrubwomen at the General Electric plant in Schenectady, New York, be included in a wage settlement even though they were not part of the larger case involving that company.[23]

When the War Labor Board closed down its work in the summer of 1919, the joint chairman for labor, Basil Manly, who had replaced Walsh, wrote Taft to praise "the fairness and open-mindedness with which you considered the cases brought before us."[24] Taft had displayed that attitude in the first and one of the most controversial episodes that the board faced. The Western Union company, which played a decisive role in communications in the era before long-distance telephones became commonplace, was facing the possibility of a strike by the Commercial Telegraphers Union of America in the spring of 1918.

The president of Western Union, Newcomb Carlton, had forbidden strikes as a condition of employment at his company, a position that the United States Supreme Court had recently upheld. The union intended to challenge the policy and sought the board's support. If Taft, Walsh, and the board sided with Western Union, their credibility with labor would vanish. If they took the union position, employers would simply ignore the board and its dictates. Walsh wanted to take a hard line with Western Union. Taft suggested instead that informal talks take place between a board member from the management side and Carlton.[25] In this instance, Taft's persuasive powers could not shake the anti-union stance of Carlton. The employer rejected all the proposals of the NWLB, and in the end the Wilson administration simply took over the telegraph industry for the war effort.

For the most part, however, Taft's conciliatory approach and case-by-case style contributed to the positive results that the board achieved for the administration. One prominent journalist, Gilson Gardner, praised the former president for his new-found affinity with labor. Gardner had been one of Theodore Roosevelt's newspaper allies a decade earlier. Now he proclaimed that Taft "is rapidly becoming popular among laboring people." If Taft should one day be nominated for the Supreme Court, Gardner continued, "the reasons which formerly made him non eligible will now be removed."[26]

Taft did not believe that his service on the War Labor Board required that he abstain from political activity in the 1918 congressional elections. His disgust with the foreign and domestic policies of the Wilson administration had intensified since the election of 1916. "The Republican party is the party of capacity and ability in the country" and thus a Republican Congress would be "more loyal" to the president and the war effort "than a Democratic Congress." Taft prepared to take to the stump once more to elect GOP members and challenge the leadership of the White House.[27]

Taft's desire to repudiate the Wilson administration led him to a public reconciliation with Theodore Roosevelt during the spring of 1918. The impetus for ending their quarrel came from the new chair of the Republican National Committee, Will H. Hays of Indiana. Elected in February 1918, Hays made it his primary task to restore party unity after the fissures that 1912 had produced. Shortly after his selection, he went to New York to "call on Mr. Roosevelt, Mr. Taft, and Mr. Hughes." Hays followed a simple philosophy. "Our party has no yesterdays," he said. "We do not care how a man voted in 1912, 1914, or 1916, nor his reasons for so doing."[28]

In that spirit, Hays approached Taft about ending the rupture with Roosevelt. If Republicans could see that feat accomplished, a powerful signal regarding party unity would galvanize the GOP faithful. Hays pushed on an open door. Taft had already sent Roosevelt a telegram of concern when his onetime friend had gone into the hospital in early February 1918.[29] Roosevelt had responded with thanks a month later as he recuperated. In his letter, Roosevelt asked Taft to read over and comment on a speech that he was to give to the Maine Republican Convention on 28 March. "Tell me anything you have to say in the way of criticism or suggestion," Roosevelt wrote.[30]

While the warm personal feelings that had existed before 1910 did not reappear, the two men now had a compelling reason for collaboration, their mutual antipathy toward Woodrow Wilson. Taft believed that Wilson had never intended to send American troops to France to fight with the Allies. As he told other correspondents, Wilson was an innate pacifist, an admirer of Lenin and the Bolsheviks in Russia, and unwilling to press the war to a final Allied victory. These conclusions, however far removed from the reality of the president's policies, pleased Roosevelt, who wrote back that "your letter is the very best exposition of Wilson's inmost soul that I have read at all."[31]

The opinions of Roosevelt and Taft about Wilson said more about their personal feelings and intense partisanship than they did about the actuality of the American war effort. Roosevelt still smarted because the president had not let him take a volunteer division

Will H. Hays. As chair of the Republican National Committee in 1918, Hays brokered a reconciliation between Taft and Roosevelt. (Library of Congress LC-FIG-hec-1877)

overseas to France. He felt this way despite the abundant evidence in 1917 and 1918 that his poor health would not have withstood the rigors of wartime generalship. Nor had Roosevelt trained in handling large groups of men in combat. These practical considerations paled before Roosevelt's conviction that he ought to have the right to die on the field of battle as an inspiration to the Allies.

For his part, Taft had long doubted Wilson's talents as a national leader and believed the worst about the president. Adding to his concerns were continuing fears about the fate of his son Charles who was now stationed in France and seeking to become an officer. Hoping for a quick Allied victory that would facilitate his dreams of a world organization and bring his son home safely, Taft let himself believe that Wilson was engaging in unpatriotic conduct as, in his mind, Democrats always did.

It was easier to take such a stance than to recognize the immense logistical challenges any president would have faced in mobilizing the nation to participate in the struggle being waged in Europe. Taft had only had to summon the full weight of the American armed forces for potential action once, in 1911, when faced with unrest in revolutionary Mexico. Deploying a mere twenty thousand troops to the Rio Grande border proved a difficult undertaking, nothing like drafting, training, and moving millions of soldiers across the Atlantic to the western front. There were legitimate criticisms to be made of the Wilson administration and its performance in wartime, but both Taft and Roosevelt went overboard in their indictment of the president.

The news that Taft and Roosevelt were once again on speaking terms galvanized the Republicans. The public moment of reconciliation occurred on 26 May 1918 in Chicago in the dining room of the Blackstone Hotel. Unlike the meeting during the Hughes campaign in 1916, this reunion was not prearranged. Taft came to the hotel at around 8:00 p.m. and was told that Roosevelt was at dinner with his party. Entering the room, Taft approached Roosevelt, who jumped to his feet. The two men shook hands, clasped each other on the shoulder, and then began "slapping each other on the back. The crowd went wild, and a cheer went up that startled them." As they sat and talked about Woodrow Wilson, reported journalists, "a six year's war was brought to a dramatic close."[32]

For understandable reasons, the Republicans hyped the reunion and the party harmony it reflected. In fact, while the two men joined in denouncing Wilson, the reconciliation was only skin deep. "You may have seen that Roosevelt and I have become reconciled. I don't know that he has changed opinion on the issues of the past, but I think we were both glad to come into friendly relations again." Roosevelt in private spoke of "Taft and his followers" in a manner that suggested continuing reservations. For the last months of Roosevelt's life, he put aside the recriminations of the past for public consumption.[33]

In July, the Republicans of New York State held an informal convention to pick their nominees for the fall election. At the suggestion of Will Hays, Roosevelt and Taft appeared on consecutive days to criticize the Wilson administration. Roosevelt sounded familiar themes about the alleged lack of White House preparations for war and the need for a more aggressive policy toward the Germans and peace terms. Taft now joined in the attack with a plea for the election of a Republican Congress. The Democrats and the president had neglected to deal with the needs of the war. "There is always a halt and a hesitation in adopting the necessary course finally entered upon." The country, Taft proclaimed, needed "a Republican Congress to call for and insist upon adequate preparation and to formulate legislation to this end. Such a Congress will in every way back up and sustain the Democratic president in winning this war."[34]

Taft spent time in Murray Bay for the rest of the summer and then returned to his War Labor Board work, his column writing, and his pleas for the election of a Republican Congress throughout the fall of 1918. His skepticism of President Wilson's good faith intensified as the military situation turned in favor of the Allies on the western front. He believed that Wilson wanted a negotiated peace settlement with the Germans that would fall short of the unconditional surrender and total victory that Taft desired. These attitudes brought him ever closer to the position of Roosevelt, Henry

Cabot Lodge, and other Republicans who wanted to see the German foe beaten into submission.

When the German government, its military position collapsing, asked the president for peace terms in October 1918, Taft joined many other Republicans and some Democrats in criticizing Wilson for not demanding "unconditional surrender of a tricky, cruel, and untrustworthy foe." For Taft the only rational goal involved taking the Allied armies through to Berlin. When the Germans produced an equivocal response to what Wilson had said, Taft applauded the president's tough reply but still remained unhappy that the White House had not come out for unconditional surrender. Even when Wilson insisted on virtual German capitulation, Taft spoke of unconditional surrender as the only realistic policy goal. He believed that Wilson had not achieved his secret longing for a negotiated peace that would leave German power in place. Taft did not analyze in any serious way the prospect of occupying a prostrate Germany for an extended period of time.[35]

Unhappy with Wilson's conduct toward the Germans, Taft received further proof of the president's political iniquity on 25 October. The White House released a statement from Wilson asking for the election of a Democratic Congress to support him during the remainder of his administration. Victory for Republican candidates "would be interpreted on the other side of the water as a repudiation of my leadership." He asserted that "it is well understood there as well as here that the Republican leaders desire not so much to support the President as to control him." The Republicans were "not in fact in sympathy with the attitude and action of the Administration."[36]

Republicans reacted with fury at what they interpreted as a presidential assault on their patriotism. Like other party members, Taft believed that the Republicans had a virtual monopoly on the capacity to govern and the true interests of the nation. To have their commitment to real American values called into question seemed intolerable. The only credible explanation for Wilson's conduct, as Taft saw it, was his secret desire to be a dictator of American politics. As Taft told his half-brother Charles, Wilson sought "autocratic power and uncontrolled will." In a speech at Portsmouth, New Hampshire, on 1 November, the former president said that "the appeal for unrestrained power is unprecedented in the annals of the country and is as unrepublican as it is unnecessary."[37]

Taft never did explain how having more Democrats in Congress would make Wilson a tyrant, but his words resonated with his fellow partisans. Charles D. Hilles told Taft that "the President makes the demand of unconditional surrender upon the Republican voters of the United States. We asked for meat and he gave us a stone." Taft joined with Theodore Roosevelt in their last act of political cooperation in the days before the election. They issued a joint manifesto they had prepared while sitting together at the Union League Club in New York. In their statement, which Taft wrote, they argued that Wilson lacked a mandate for anything other than unconditional surrender, and they charged that a Democratic Congress would simply endorse whatever Wilson recommended. "We urge all Americans who are Americans first to vote for a Republican Congress."[38] The union of two former presidents against the policies of an incumbent was unprecedented.

The renewed Taft-Roosevelt harmony masked persistent differences between the two men over the direction of a possible peace settlement. Taft still adhered to the program of the League to Enforce Peace, while Roosevelt continued to have doubts about the efficacy of any such scheme. In August, Roosevelt had told Taft that he could only accept existence of a League of Nations as an addition to universal military training, a formulation that Taft accepted. The assurances lacked a good deal of candor. As Roosevelt told Albert J. Beveridge in October, "mine is merely a platonic expression, designed to let Taft and his followers to get over without too much trouble, and also to prevent any accusation that we are ourselves merely Prussian militarists." Even as his health declined and the end of his life neared, Roosevelt patronized his one-time comrade.[39]

Taft had to face this issue in the days just before the election when the Democratic governor of North Carolina, Thomas W. Bickett, pointed out how Roosevelt assailed the president and "the basic principles of the League to Enforce Peace." Taft responded that "the truth is that the President does not favor our League to Enforce Peace." Roosevelt in Taft's mind "has come around to favoring the League to Enforce Peace, providing it does not mean universal disarmament." Roosevelt had thus persuaded Taft of his good faith on the peace issue, and then died before the differences between the two men could be revealed in the ensuing battle about the League of Nations.

When the Democrats lost control of Congress, one of Taft's Connecticut friends wrote that "the American Kaiser has received the rebuke he so richly deserved." On election day the voters gave the Republicans a decisive victory. They retook control of the House for the first time since 1910, and they managed a narrow two-vote majority in the Senate. Wilson's capacity to write a peace settlement without consulting the opposition no longer existed. Taft credited Wilson's "singularly inept address to the people" with bringing out otherwise apathetic Republican voters. With Wilson limited to two terms by the informal tradition that then dominated American politics, prospects looked good for the Republicans in 1920. Now sixty-one years old, Taft worried that time was running out on his Supreme Court chances. Nonetheless, a Republican president in 1921 might turn his way if Chief Justice Edward D. White, in his mid-seventies, should retire or die.[40]

With the war over, attention in Washington turned to the impending peace conference in Paris and the role that President Wilson might play in that assembly. Taft's involvement in the struggle over the peace treaty and the League of Nations dominated his career in 1919. Before that occurred, Theodore Roosevelt died. His activities against Wilson and for the Republicans in 1918 came amid mounting evidence of the former president's failing health. In the month following the victory for the Grand Old Party in the elections, Roosevelt was back in a New York hospital for a variety of crippling ailments. He returned home to Oyster Bay in mid-December and died in his sleep on 6 January 1919.

Roosevelt's funeral took place two days later, and Taft attended to see his old friend and one-time rival laid to rest. The reporter for the *New York Tribune* watched Taft as the brief ceremony progressed.

"Near the front of the church, on the left, sat William Howard Taft. His mouth was twitching and several times he brushed tears from his eyes."[41] As Taft wrote his wife that evening, his original seating in the church was "in a pew behind the family in the same seat with the family servants." At that point, Archibald Roosevelt intervened and said: "You're a dear personal friend and must come up further." Taft sat behind Vice President Thomas Riley Marshall, representing Woodrow Wilson, and in front of the members of Congress, including Roosevelt's oldest friend, Senator Henry Cabot Lodge, "his face contorted by suppressed grief."[42]

Taft's biographer, Henry F. Pringle, portrays Taft at the time of Roosevelt's death as ready to do "the gracious thing" but not grief-stricken at his friend's death. He noted that Taft went to the theater on the evening of 8 January. The suggestion that Taft was a mite callous and insincere in his emotions at Roosevelt's death seems overdone. The funeral had ended, Taft was back in New York, and life went on. One should give Taft some credit for grieving in his own way. As he told Anna Roosevelt Cowles, Roosevelt's sister, two years later, "I want to say to you how glad I am that Theodore and I came together after that long painful interval. Had he died in a hostile state of mind toward me, I would have mourned the fact all my life. I loved him always and cherished his memory."[43]

A thorough, careful study of the Taft-Roosevelt relationship from the early 1890s through Roosevelt's death and beyond has yet to be written. A sentimental, emotional man, Taft succeeded in getting beyond the recriminations and passions of their rupture in 1912. In his written eulogy for the dead leader, he called his enemy and friend "the most interesting and the most brilliant personality in American public life since Lincoln."[44]

During the rest of his life, Taft resisted efforts to have him write about his relationship with Theodore Roosevelt at any length. Occupied with his busy schedule from 1913 to 1921 and then chief justice after July 1921, Taft never had time nor the inclination to sum up his feelings about the man who had helped to make him president and then defeated his reelection bid.

It is interesting to speculate on what would have happened had

Roosevelt lived to run for president in 1920. As the president again, what would Roosevelt have done when Chief Justice White died in 1921? While there had been a political reconciliation, the two men had not recreated the personal rapport that had once existed. Would a newly elected President Roosevelt have wished to reward Taft's conservatism and forget the passions of 1912 and 1916? Of course, it never came to pass and Taft would find his way to the court on his own after two years of balancing his desire for a League of Nations with his enduring fidelity to the Republican Party.

6

THE LEAGUE OR THE PARTY

The war ended one week after the results of the 1918 congressional election came in. Thoughts in political Washington turned at once to the shape of the peace settlement, the role of the president in negotiating a treaty, and the reaction of the new Republican Congress to whatever Woodrow Wilson proposed. Despite his greater tolerance for organized labor while on the War Labor Board, William Howard Taft had in no respect become a progressive during the conflict. On two areas of social conflict, however, he had modified his beliefs in light of his wartime experience.

Despite his own abstinence from alcohol, Taft had long been suspicious of prohibition as an answer to the nation's moral dilemmas. He did not believe that liquor control could be sustained. More important, he feared that giving the federal government the "needed police power and patronage, normally parochial, would disturb the proper constitutional balance between federal and state governments [so] as to imperil the stability of the Union." Since the voters and Congress by early 1919 had adopted national prohibition, however, Taft was "in favor of the strongest kind of a law for its enforcement." Such a stringent program of regulation would in time demonstrate the impracticality of prohibition as a panacea for the problems that liquor created for society.[1]

The war also shifted Taft's position on women's suffrage. As president and afterward, he had believed that voting was a matter for the states to decide, and he had not favored national action. He blamed the loss in 1916 in part "on the emotional votes of women." His perception that men in power seemed indifferent to the danger of future wars led him to the conclusion that "modern progress requires that women's influence be allowed to exert itself through the ballot." While the practical effect would "dilute the electorate by introducing a good deal of ignorance into it in greater proportion than now exists and the still greater threat of inexperience," on social and labor issues, women "would speak with a force that could not be neglected and would make the timorous politicians jump." Taft had not really altered his dismissive view of women and their intellects, but he saw their votes as both a practical reality and a potential asset for his side of the political debate.[2]

In late November 1918, a possibility arose for Taft's life to move in a nonpolitical and fresh direction. He received a proposal from Harry Frazee, owner of the then world champion baseball team, the Boston Red Sox, and Harry N. Hempstead of the New York Giants. They invited Taft to become, in effect, the commissioner of major league baseball. Within the sport there were serious divisions over the future course of baseball after World War I, and Taft emerged as a figure who might heal the rifts.[3]

News of the offer occasioned a flurry of speculation about Taft's intentions. The former president made it clear that he would only serve as a judge on legal matters and would not "in any way take part in the management of their associations." In the end, after further public airing of the responsibilities he would be assuming, Taft decided to shun baseball. He became convinced that Frazee and Hempstead had misled him about their proposal. "What they had in mind," he said, "was to substitute me for the present national commission . . . I could not consider such an offer under any circumstances." It was only after the Black Sox scandal of 1919 and other problems with baseball that the owners would turn to Kenesaw Mountain Landis to serve as commissioner during the period between the two world wars.[4]

Taft remained on the National War Labor Board until June 1919 and continued his involvement with the Red Cross. Most of this time went to the League to Enforce Peace and the struggle over the

League of Nations. In pursuing the goal of a world organization to keep the peace, Taft had to contend with the pervasive dislike, not to say hatred, among his fellow Republicans for the president and all his works. Taft's cooperation with the White House over the peace treaty during the first half of 1919 aroused suspicion and resentment within the higher reaches of the Grand Old Party.

Wilson's aloof and condescending political style had done much on its own to evoke Republican animosity to him since he had become president in 1913. In dealing with his opponents, Wilson could be tricky and even dishonest. His slippery language and his practice of "grazing the truth" infuriated Republicans. Granting all these weaknesses in Wilson's character and performance in office, the feelings that Republicans such as Henry Cabot Lodge and his Senate colleagues displayed toward Wilson went beyond resentment and anger and verged on the pathological.

Wilson's personality thus became a significant aspect of the opposition to him in 1919–1920. The animus that Henry Cabot Lodge felt toward him is well known. In 1915, he said that he "never expected to hate any one in politics with the hatred I feel towards Wilson." Lodge believed that his feelings were reciprocated. "With the exception of Roosevelt there is no one the President dislikes more than he dislikes me." Hiram Johnson of California, new to the Senate as a Republican in 1918, observed: "All of the Republicans and many of the Democrats violently hate and detest him."[5]

Beyond their personal animosity, Republicans disliked the way in which the president had twice defeated them for the White House. They were convinced that a united Grand Old Party would have beaten Wilson if there had not been the three-way race in 1912. The victory over Hughes in 1916 they attributed to the bogus claim that "he kept us out of war," which Wilson knew he could not sustain. Believing that they were the natural governing party, Republicans saw Democrats tainted with treason, first dating back to the Civil War, and now with Bolshevism from Russia. Republican senators believed that Wilson was illegitimate and unfit to hold office. Anyone who consorted with him, as Taft proposed to do, ran the risk of being branded a heretic, what a later generation

Henry Cabot Lodge. Taft and Lodge had never liked each other much, and they clashed over their differing views of the Treaty of Versailles. (Library of Congress LC-USZ62-36185)

would term a Republican In Name Only (RINO). Since his Republican credentials were, in Taft's mind, beyond reproach, the former president did not always realize the suspicions he stirred among his partisan colleagues when he praised the League of Nations, offered suggestions to the White House, and criticized his fellow Republicans over their anti-league stances.

Republicans bristled when the White House announced that President Wilson would attend the impending peace conference in Paris as the head of the American delegation. Several constitutional questions arose. Theodore Roosevelt had gone to Panama in 1906 and Taft himself had crossed into Mexico in 1909 from El Paso to greet then-president Porfirio Díaz. No president had challenged the informal restraint on the chief executive leaving the borders of the United States with a prolonged trip to Europe.[6]

The Republicans saw an immediate opening. They claimed that with Wilson out of the country the presidency would be vacant. Vice President Thomas Riley Marshall should assume power in Wilson's absence. Taft's former attorney general George Wickersham attributed the situation to Wilson's "whisperings of personal ambition," which would lead to "new, uncertain and perhaps dangerous questions of constitutional right and power." Senator Lawrence Y. Sherman offered a resolution to declare the presidency vacant if Wilson was absent from the United States because "the whole American atmosphere that ought to surround the President is lost."[7]

In his newspaper columns, Taft rebutted these Republican arguments from his own experiences in the White House. He saw no constitutional reasons why Wilson should not go to Paris. "There is not the slightest doubt that he has full power in this regard," Taft added, and remembering Roosevelt's visit to Panama and his own foray into Mexico in 1909, "there is no occasion for criticism or worry." Taft deprecated the Republican efforts to make political trouble for the president on this issue. The pleasantly surprised Secretary of War Newton D. Baker told Wilson, who was now on his way to Paris, that Taft had "a lucid interval" and had produced "a very sensible article" in defense of the president's course.[8]

When the president selected the diplomatic delegation that accompanied him to Paris, Taft's name did not appear. According to the former president, he had been considered for a slot on the Wilson team. "I have been advised since, from the entourage of the President" that had he not coauthored the appeal for a Republican Congress with Theodore Roosevelt, "or had I not questioned his fourteen points, I might have been privileged to represent the country on the Commission." He did not believe the rumor. The only way he would have been selected, he told Theodore Roosevelt, was if the choice had been "limited to the two ex-Presidents." In any event, he informed another friend, "it would be impossible for me to serve under a gentleman who insists on exact obedience and declines the slightest opportunity for consultation or suggestion."[9]

Taft doubted this comforting assurance from White House insiders. It had little basis in fact. When a newspaper editor suggested Taft's name to Wilson, he received a tart reply: "I appreciate both the motive and advice of your telegraphic message, but must frankly say that I would not dare take Mr. Taft. I have lost all confidence in his character." He was more friendly to the League to Enforce Peace because it was "now purged of Taftism." But the president gave out an interview later in December in which he said he had never endorsed the program of the League to Enforce Peace. Such a statement of course undercut Taft's position with that body.[10]

Taft brushed the president's criticism of the league aside. Looking back to Wilson's speech of 27 May 1916 addressing the League to Enforce Peace, he asserted that those in the audience could not "escape the conviction that he was in general and almost specific accord not only with the purposes but the methods of the league." For Taft that meant some reliance on international courts. Wilson questioned whether such an approach could work. That point would remain a source of division for the two men throughout the ensuing battle over the League of Nations itself.

Despite these differences, Taft became part of an elaborate campaign by his League to Enforce Peace to build support for Wilson's vision during February 1919. The leaders of the league decided to hold ten regional meetings during the period from 5 February to

28 February. Taft was the leading orator and his appearances attracted large audiences and enthusiastic applause. Even before the league campaign began, the former president had started his personal appeals. He spoke before the National Geographic Society in Washington on 17 January. "It is a narrow view of our international duty which would prevent our keeping the rest of the world out of the danger of war." Since the country had become "the world's greatest power," it followed that "we should not wish to avoid the responsibility which that entails upon us."[11]

On one level, Taft and the League to Enforce Peace could point to obvious signs that their campaign in February 1919 reflected strong popular support for the creation of an international organization to maintain peace. Writing from Stockton, California, on 21 February, he noted the attendance at six of the nine peace congresses that the league had sponsored. Taft concluded that "the public mind favors the plan and does not recoil at the proposal that this country shall bear its share of the burden needed to give a bite to the league." At the same time, he and his league colleagues thought that it "would be a tragedy in the history of civilization if the Senate can be influenced by the protests and narrow views of a small number of senators who have expressed themselves to defeat this grand covenant of peace, the unanimous agreement of the representatives of fourteen nations facing not a theory, but a real and fateful crisis for the world."[12]

Taft was finding out what Woodrow Wilson would learn later in his speaking tour during the fall of 1919. Demonstrations of popular support for some kind of league of nations had little direct influence on the opinions of the senators who would in the end decide the fate of this issue. While President Wilson was in Paris during the months of January and February, Republican senators opposed to his policies had hardened in their dislike of what he was proposing to commit the United States to overseas. The most outspoken was Senator William E. Borah of Idaho who said, "If the Savior of mankind should revisit the earth and declare for a League of Nations I would be opposed to it." Other Republicans were not so vocal, but there remained a large degree of suspicion of the president's motives and his good faith toward the upper house.[13]

The contours of the fight over the proposed League of Nations became evident when Wilson announced on 14 February 1919 the outline of the new organization to the Paris Peace Conference. The statement contained the key points that would frame the debate for the remainder of the year. The most notable, of course, was Article X that pledged member states of the new league to band together to resist efforts, by force if necessary, to compromise the independence and territorial integrity of any of its members. Taft at once raised his voice in praise of what Wilson had done. "President Wilson is to be warmly congratulated that the league of nations which he promised to the harassed Allied peoples in his messages and addresses and has urged before the conference has taken such a form." To the opponents of the league in the Senate, the former president said that many of them "are merely destructive critics and are not in search of a solution of the difficulty."[14]

Taft recognized that Wilson was going to have a large task in persuading enough senators to obtain a two-thirds majority for the new League of Nations. The eventual peace treaty still had to be hammered out in Paris. After announcing the League Covenant, the president returned home to the United States to deal with the end of the lame-duck congressional session then drawing to a close. Taft sought to help Wilson sell the new league to the American people, but he recognized the obstacles that lay ahead. In an impassioned letter to Gus Karger on 22 February, he laid out his new support for women's suffrage on the basis of the personal and political weaknesses of Republicans in the Senate as a group. In the process, he also reflected on his uncertain standing among the members of his party's leadership.

His sympathy for women voting, he told Karger, became stronger "when I think of the vicious narrowness of Reed, the explosive ignorance of Poindexter, the ponderous Websterian language and lack of stamina of Borah, the vanity of Lodge as an old diplomatic hand on the Foreign Relations Committee, the selfishness, laziness and narrow lawyer-like acuteness of Knox, the emptiness and sly partisanship of Hale, with the utter nothingness of Fall, in the face of this world crisis."[15]

Taft assured Karger that "I am not drunk or wild but am only roused to the critical situation in world affairs that those who gather around the council board in Paris knew, and that these barking critics do not seem to realize. It is in their American selfishness, their American littleness, blinding them to real interests of the nation, as well as of the world, that rouses me." In the course of his impassioned missive, which would have blighted his hopes for future preferment among Republicans had it become public knowledge, Taft also addressed how he was perceived within his own party.

He invoked the presence of Republican National Chairman Will H. Hays as one of the potential critics. "I can see that little head of Hays wagging over the errors I have made from a political standpoint." More than that were the comments of "the wiseacres" who were saying of Taft, or so he thought, "that shows what defeated the party in 1912, and here's a repetition of it. Weren't the Progressives justified in breaking off? Taft's loyalty to the party was always weak. Now thank God he is out of it." With mock tolerance, Taft told Karger that having incurred "this condemnation by so noble a body as the Republicans of the Senate," he faced "a sad fate, but I must bear it. Goodbye."[16]

The letter to Karger reflected Taft's uneasiness at the damage his pro-Wilson position was doing among his fellow Republicans. For the moment, however, he remained in public sympathy with the president and the new League of Nations idea. As Wilson left Paris and headed homeward, he sought Taft's support at one of the appearances he intended to make on behalf of his foreign policy idea. The president was scheduled to speak in New York on 4 March, and Taft agreed to share the platform with him. "I am glad to have the opportunity of emphasizing the transcendental importance and the non-partisan character of the issue in respect to the proposed League of Nations by speaking with you in New York next Tuesday night," Taft wired back to the president.[17]

The atmospherics of the event on 4 March 1919 linked Taft to the president's program. The two men entered the stage at the Metropolitan Opera House arm in arm amid a fanfare of bugles.

Standing to Wilson's left, Taft asked: "Am I on your right side, Mr. President?" Wilson responded: "I hadn't noticed which side you are on, but I am certain you are on the right side." The reporters said that Taft was in evening dress, "rotund and hearty." Governor Al Smith then said, introducing Taft, that "The Most High has given us two champions to guide us. He has given us Moses." Taft chuckled at this comparison and then plunged into his fifty-eight-minute address.[18]

Taft did not serve as a cheerleader for President Wilson. The editors of the *Outlook* said "he never made a finer or more magnetic speech," but it was the response of a gifted attorney addressing the criticisms of opposing counsel. Point by point, Taft spoke to the attacks already leveled against Wilson's brainchild. He defended the provisions about disarmament, endorsed the language about arbitrating differences among nations, and rebutted the idea that Article X would lead the United States into wars without the consent of Congress.[19]

Senatorial attacks on the league, Taft added, lacked practical suggestions about what the nation should do to meet "the threatening specter of Bolshevism" and potential world disorder. The league would not threaten the Monroe Doctrine, but Taft did say that a formal recognition of the doctrine in a revised treaty would be wise. In sum, there would be no abridgment of national sovereignty in this and other areas that the United States did not agree to in a voluntary manner. Of course, like any sovereign nation, it could change its mind as circumstances warranted. At the end, Taft provided a rhetorical bow to Senator Lodge by saying that the president might find "useful suggestions" in a recent speech the Massachusetts senator had made. He added, however, that Lodge "and other critics have misunderstood the purpose and meaning of the words used." For Lodge, an aggressive opponent of Wilson, such honeyed phrases would not do much to assuage his dislike of the league.[20]

Taft concluded that "the League Covenant should be in the Treaty of Peace." The huge crowd cheered his remarks before Wilson arose to offer his affirmation of the league as part of the peace settlement. Taft wrote to his son Robert: "I dealt with the League and he with generalities." Since the president still had to go back to Paris to finish negotiations on the terms of the treaty, it would have been unwise for him to have matched the specific points in Taft's speech. In any event, this tumultuous public moment marked the acme of the cooperation that Wilson and Taft achieved in the battle over the league.[21]

While Taft was not always the shrewdest observer of the political scene, he could see that Wilson's vision of the League of Nations was in difficulty with the Senate in early March. The day before Taft and the president spoke in New York, Senator Lodge had circulated his "Round Robin" resolution in the upper house. That document, signed by thirty or endorsed by thirty-nine senators, declared that the League of Nations in the form "now proposed by the peace conference should not be accepted by the United States." If these senators voted that way on the treaty itself, a two-thirds majority to approve the pact would be unattainable.[22]

In his New York address, Wilson had said that when he returned with the treaty Americans would find "so many threads of the treaty tied to the Covenant that you cannot dissect the Covenant from the treaty without destroying the whole vital structure." The president could make good on that promise because he was negotiating the treaty in Paris. He could not guarantee that the Senate, once in Republican hands, would approve his handiwork. Fearful of such an outcome, Taft wrote him in mid-March to ask "if he may cable you direct, for your consideration only, some suggestions about which he has been thinking a great deal, and which he would like to have you consider." Taft assured the president that his proposed ideas did not look "to the change of the structure of the League" but were designed to address objections "in the minds of conscientious Americans" who had fears that "could be removed without any considerable change of language." Wilson agreed and urged Taft to send along the proposed alterations.[23]

While Taft did so, within the League to Enforce Peace he faced opposition to his statements about the president and the covenant. On 18 March, the *New York Sun* reported that individuals within the league disliked the Wilsonian approach as "the surrender of

American sovereignty as a condition to the formation of such an association of nations." The league issued a statement denying that such a split existed: "There is no truth in the report that serious differences of opinion among officers of the league have threatened to split the organization." The extent of division within the league remained hazy, but the airing of the dispute indicated the fragility of Taft's base among the league's members.[24]

Because it would have shaken the Republican creed that had defined his life, Taft blinked at a simple fact. His party was never going to agree to a League of Nations that Woodrow Wilson had conceived and favored. The hatred for the president that pulsed through the Grand Old Party meant that any attempt at compromise would fail. Since Wilson wanted the League of Nations on his own terms or not at all, the Republicans could always say that but for the president's stubbornness it might have succeeded. By seeing to it that their positions never satisfied Wilson's criteria, Lodge and his colleagues were able to shift the onus for the failure of the League of Nations onto the president. In his later years, Taft continued to believe that it was all Wilson's fault that the league had faltered.

Taft sent his suggested alterations to the president in March 1919 in good faith. They were constructive and thoughtful, designed to meet the criticisms from Republicans about the weaknesses of the treaty. They included: a specific time limit of ten years on how long the league would exist before nations could withdraw with two years' notice; a requirement of unanimity for important decisions; and, most important, specific language to safeguard the Monroe Doctrine. Domestic questions such as immigration policy, especially regarding Asian newcomers from China and Japan, would not come under league jurisdiction. Wilson proceeded to obtain concessions from his negotiating partners. The most difficult to secure involved the Monroe Doctrine. Taft told the White House: "Monroe clause eminently satisfactory." If Taft reflected Republican sentiment, gaining these concessions would, in Wilson's mind, signal Republican acceptance of both the league and the treaty.[25]

In fact, Taft's thinking lagged well behind the pace of Republican thinking about the league in general. The GOP Senate hierarchy did not see him as a trustworthy colleague. Frank Brandegee, a Connecticut Republican lawmaker with a serious drinking problem, accused Elihu Root of a willingness "to bend in the middle or truckle to Wilson & Taft," as if both men had identical views. Henry Cabot Lodge wrote to Henry White on 8 April to say, "You need have no apprehensions about Mr. Taft being the Republican candidate for the Presidency. He never had any chance, and if he ever did it would now be less than it was. He has supported the League in his own fashion" and, Lodge concluded, "these oscillations have not strengthened him with the country."[26]

During a debate about the League of Nations, William E. Borah underscored what he and other Republicans thought of Taft. The Democrats had taken to praising Taft at regular intervals because he approved of the league and stood by Wilson. In the midst of one of these oratorical plaudits for Taft, Borah observed: "Oh, you Democrats, you think a lot of Mr. Taft right now. You have a lot of respect for him. You pay him the same respect that is shown when traffic in the street stops to let the dead pass by."[27] If Wilson ever thought that Taft could deliver Republican votes in the Senate, it illustrated how little he understood the opposition to his presidency. If Taft thought he could cooperate with Wilson without damage to his standing as a Republican, he was very naive.

Taft was pleased when Wilson released the revised covenant to the public on 26 April 1919. He now thought that the Republicans should seize the moment and announce their approval of the pact. "If they were wise, they would now fall in with the idea that by their objections they brought about these amendments and thus helped him to formulate the treaty and that they are entitled to the credit of making the treaty acceptable so that it can be ratified."[28] Taft soon learned that no such scenario could exist in the political climate of the spring of 1919. He thought that his Republican colleagues would "find more and more disagreeable the charge made by the Democrats and by Wilson that they are holding up a return to normal times." In fact, Lodge, Elihu Root, and Will Hays thought that the tide was running in their favor, and they saw no reason to change their course of obstructing Wilson.[29]

Taft found himself more and more in a political box. He was a sincere exponent of the Treaty of Versailles and wanted it ratified in the form Wilson had crafted in Paris in March and April 1919. It was becoming evident, however, that the treaty in that form could never win enough Republican votes to secure ratification. For Taft to hold out against the Republican majority in his party would risk his future on the Supreme Court in the event of a GOP president being elected in 1920. A warning from former senator Jonathan Bourne of Oregon, president of the Republican Publicity Association, illustrated what party members thought. In a mid-June statement, Bourne said that "Mr. Taft's mental gyrations since the covenant of the league became the leading issue before the country have caused his countrymen to stand aghast, and his friends to marvel at the change in the man." Taft's mental processes were now "truly sad."[30]

During the months of May and June 1919, the political tide ran against Wilson and the league. Because he had to make concessions to the European nations to secure the changes that Taft and others wanted in the league, the peace treaty became tougher on Germany, with reparations for war damages and other stern measures. These alterations eroded support for Wilson among progressive Democrats and those on the left in general. Their criticisms fed disillusion with the treaty in the country at large. Meanwhile, Lodge had persuaded Elihu Root to write again about his criticisms regarding the league and Article X. Root's insistence that Article X had to be rejected offered a rallying point for Republicans in the Senate. "It is perfectly evident at this moment," wrote Henry Cabot Lodge, "that the Republican majority in the Senate is practically solid for the Root reservations."[31]

As Wilson prepared to return to the United States after completing work on the league and the treaty, Taft advised him to base his oratory on the merits of the pact and the need for its speedy ratification. "I hope sincerely he will not attack the Republican senators," he told Joe Tumulty. "His appeal will be much more influential if he pleads his cause and does not attack the opposition." In his remarks to the Senate upon his return, Wilson took the advice of Taft and some of the president's fellow Democrats and did not attack Republicans by name or party.[32]

At some point in early July 1919, at the urging of Will Hays, Taft began to rethink his position on amendments and reservations to the peace treaty. Friends such as his former secretary Charles D. Hilles were telling him that "every present indication points to the ratification of the Treaty, but not until after some reservations had been adopted."[33] By this time it was summer, and Taft had repaired to Murray Bay where he heard from Will Hays on 9 July. The two men talked about the possibility of framing reservations that would satisfy the Republicans and secure ratification.

Taft had great faith in his ability to use his legal skills to achieve a resolution of this controversy. He also assumed that the men he dealt with shared his ultimate goal of getting the treaty through the Senate. Once again, Taft believed that he might bridge the gap between his party and the president. Why he thought he could do this, in light of the gulf that already existed between the two sides, remains a mystery. An impulsive man, Taft thought that as an ex-president he could succeed where others had failed. In fact by framing reservations as he did, he embarrassed himself and hurt the cause of ratification.

The wily Hays led Taft to believe that they shared the same goal, ultimate ratification of the treaty. The Republican chairman sought a consensus within the GOP behind ratification only with reservations. He needed Taft to be on board with such a proposal. The former president wavered. He had told his wife that "it may be that Root's letter may suggest a compromise." Taft did not enjoy being away from the mainstream of his party. He also knew that too much independence might deprive him of preferment when the Republicans regained the White House. By mid-1919, the prospects for the party to win in 1920 seemed to brighten daily.[34]

Taft went ahead with composing his letters to Hays even though his New York brother, lawyer Henry Waters Taft, warned him against hasty action. "Murray Bay is pretty far removed from this atmosphere, and we are just a bit concerned here that you should not answer too quickly suggestions coming from those who have been recently engaged in unmeasured denunciations of the League and scarcely less violent denunciations of you." Believing that Hays was "working with me for this compromise and not giving away anything in advance," Taft went ahead and wrote up the proposed reservations for confidential submission to key senators.[35]

For a man who had been president and active in American politics for more than two decades, William Howard Taft could be very gullible. He believed that he could reverse his long-standing position against reservations in letters to senators and still keep the matter quiet simply by marking his missives as "confidential." It did not occur to him that in the super-heated atmosphere of Washington in the summer of 1919, the substance of his letters conveyed explosive national news. The most prominent Republican in favor of the League of Nations and the proposed peace treaty now endorsed reservations to the treaty. Thus he went to work sublime in the confidence that he could change his mind in private and no one would leak what he had done. If Taft believed that gentlemen did not make public their private correspondence, he was about to receive an abrupt shock.

The elements of Taft's proposals consisted of six major points. The United States could withdraw from the league after two years without penalty or obligation. Self-governing colonies and dominions were barred from the league council at the same time as the imperial nation, such as Great Britain itself. Article X would become only an advisory element. Tariff and immigration issues would be outside the purview of the league. The United States would serve as the sole judge of the Monroe Doctrine. Finally, the United States could drop out of the league after ten years and escape its obligations under Article X.[36]

In his letters to Hays, copies of which soon circulated in Washington, Taft leveled a number of criticisms at President Wilson for being too partisan. He also indicted Wilson for rejecting the proposal of the League to Enforce Peace for "an international court and the settlement of justiciable questions." While retaining Article X was necessary "in order to stabilize the world," reservations should be added to get the treaty through the Senate.

Taft argued that the president should have taken Elihu Root and two members of the Senate Foreign Relations Committee with him to Paris. Then all the problems might have been avoided. Taft clung to the odd belief that Republicans in Paris, as team players, would have muted their criticisms of the president's handiwork. He never regarded working with the White House, either on the National War Labor Board or as an adviser on league matters, as any kind of bar to chastising the president in public. While Wilson should probably have done more to consult with prominent Republicans, he could well have concluded that GOP members wanted to have things both ways, to the president's political detriment.[37]

The Taft letters caused a sensation in the nation's capital. Reporters noted that the former president, hitherto one of the president's strongest backers, had "abandoned the bandwagon" of those who sought ratification without reservations and now sought changes "more radical in some respects than what Mr. Root has suggested." In fact, the leaked letters appeared even before they reached Will Hays himself. In his missives to the Republican chairman, Taft had said: "I wish to avoid injury to the cause by complete self-effacement if that will help." Instead, he had broken with the administration, embarrassed the League to Enforce Peace, and failed to advance the interest of ratification.[38]

Copies of Taft's letters reached the White House, possibly through a Republican senator, as early as July 18. Speaking to a British diplomat on that date, the president derided Taft. "He complained rather bitterly that Mr. Taft is weakening [in] his support and now thinks there ought to be reservations to the League." Gus Karger did not know of Wilson's anger. "Thus far," he told Taft, "I have no definite information to the effect that the President has indicated willingness to accept interpretations." Since people in Washington recognized that Karger was both a Republican and close to Taft, it was unlikely that Wilson would have told him much beyond generalities.[39]

The immediate repercussions of Taft's initiative left the parliamentary situation regarding the treaty unchanged, but shredded the ex-president's credibility. "The Taft letters will have no effect in the Senate," said William E. Borah. "The only effect will be among the people throughout the country who will believe that Mr. Taft has flopped."[40] The elders of his own party disliked his initiative, particularly because he had written to senators on both sides of the issue. "The idea of Mr. Taft assuming any functions of intermediary for the Republican opponents of the League in dealing with its advocates was resented by the Republican leaders."[41]

At the White House, Taft's letters "caused dismay" though officials there would not speak with the press. The verdict was that "Taft's action seemed to create an impression of weakness on his part, a readiness to surrender his own political convictions to 'the exigencies, personal, partisan and political,' which he says must be recognized in the present situation." The sense of Taft retreating and conceding points to the opponents of the League of Nations especially irritated the men around the president.[42]

One of those key White House aides was Secretary of War Newton D. Baker. He read Taft's statements in the morning newspaper and called them "the *ne plus ultra!*" He dismissed how Taft had criticized Wilson because "he cannot understand anyone having a higher motive" than himself. Baker did note that Taft's comments about other Republicans were scathing in their assumption that GOP members had to be stroked to get them to do "their sworn duty by their country! Surely nobody ever said so derogating a thing before about the statesmen of his own party and he says it with his hands flat on the table and his head turned, so that he does not know he has said it."[43]

Once the letters to Hays became public, Taft had to engage in what a later generation would call "damage control." He told one senator: "I tried to keep my suggestions confidential but they seem to have been given publicity. I don't know that it makes much difference except that it may be used to claim that the supporters of the League are losing faith." He still professed himself ready to vote for the league without amendments and alleged that his proposed reservations would not have any practical impact on the working of the organization once launched. Friendly senators told him that they could "discover no change in the Senate situation" in the wake of his letters.[44]

Taft devoted a good deal of his time in the immediate aftermath of the release of the letters to finding out how the leak had happened. He asked the United Press to make clear that his letters had been marked "confidential" and had been disclosed against his will. Gus Karger and his press colleagues speculated about who the culprit might be. One name mentioned was Henry Cabot Lodge. It did not really matter. Taft had sent out political dynamite to any number of partisan Republicans. The letters proclaimed the defection of one of the president's few apparent Republican allies. In an "anything goes" atmosphere to beat Wilson, the Taft letters gave the league's opponents an irresistible chance to win a public relations war.

One of Taft's Republican critics, George H. Moses of New Hampshire, speculated in the Senate that what Taft had done might "make the promoters of the League to Enforce Peace, of which he is the head, feel that he has given them grounds for thinking that he has made them spend money under false pretenses." It wasn't quite that overt but it came close. The League to Enforce Peace acted to reiterate their commitment to unconditional ratification on 31 July. The executive committee adopted a resolution favoring unconditional action by the Senate. Then it added a jab at Taft: "The Executive Committee, in adopting the foregoing resolution, is in accord with the position of its President, the Hon. William Howard Taft, who declared in his letter to Chairman Hays, that he favors unconditional ratification of the Treaty and Covenant and would vote therefore were he a member of the United States Senate." When reporters caught up with Taft in Chicago and asked him about the action of his league, he responded, "I think I have talked enough on this subject."[45]

After Taft's actions, the League to Enforce Peace had to decide what to do about its president. Taft admitted that he had acted in haste. "The truth is I was too full of desire to reach a compromise which should give us the League without weakening it, and made my suggestions without sufficient consultation with others, isolated as I am from easy discussion." He offered to resign, and the league gave serious consideration to that step. An internal report indicated that the only logical course was to have Taft step down. A. Lawrence Lowell persuaded other members of the league's executive committee not to accept Taft's resignation. However, the difficulties in Taft's position emerged during the month of August 1919. He refused to repeat his previous commitment to ratification without reservations and in September told the league it could not use his name in fund-raising.[46]

Taft did not sever his connection with the League to Enforce Peace, but his relations with it after July 1919 became strained. He and William H. Short, the league secretary, found themselves at odds over strategy. Short wanted to have Taft's imprimatur on the substantive appeals for donations that the league sent out. These materials adhered to the league's position in favor of ratification without reservations. Having come out for reservations, Taft did not want to be seen as endorsing ratification absent the changes he had proposed. As he told Short on 25 August, "I am very much out of patience with your methods of doing business and using my name to secure others to sign a manifesto which I do not myself approve." Taft said that "we shall never get this treaty through unless we encourage the mild reservationist Republicans to keep up their organization and secure enough votes, and the beating of tom toms and demand for ratification without reservations made part of the instrument of ratification will only aggravate the situation and minimize the chances of the treaty."[47]

At some level, the common purpose of the members of the League to Enforce Peace had disappeared and would never return. From this point, the organization lost most of its influence and became only a subsidiary player in the negotiations taking place in the Senate. The perception grew that it was influenced by its Democratic members to serve the interest of Wilson and the White House. What had begun as a noble effort on Taft's part in 1915 to pursue world peace had descended into partisan rancor. When it came down to it, Taft's Republican allegiance trumped his previous devotion to the pursuit of a treaty without reservations.[48]

7

TAFT AND THE TREATY DEFEATED

William Howard Taft's public endorsement of reservations to the Treaty of Versailles in July 1919 ended whatever slight influence he had within the administration of Woodrow Wilson. Gus Karger informed him of the abrupt shift in how the White House perceived Taft. "Joe Tumulty is displeased with you; from the greatest statesman America had produced in decades, you have degenerated—well, you know the polite term." The break with the president did not, however, make Taft more influential with the Republican leadership in the Senate. They paid scant attention to Taft's columns in the Philadelphia *Public Ledger* and ignored his frequent speeches around the country. A month after his letters to Hays had appeared, a Republican newspaper reported that "the high distinction of the author of these numerous and voluminous emanations counts for nothing apparently in Congress."[1]

Since Taft continued to proclaim his desire to have the treaty ratified as the president had brought it back from France, his support for Republican reservations seemed expedient and insincere. Taft had abandoned a well-defined position and earned only polite disdain from his GOP colleagues. The Democrats, for their part, stopped praising his support for the president's position. As the *Washington Times* put it, there would be no union of Wilson and Taft over the league. "Alas for human frailty. It was so beautiful when Mr. Wilson and Mr. Taft, cheek to cheek, murmured peace at the Metropolitan Opera House."[2]

In the weeks following the disclosure of his Hays letters, Taft continued to speak out on the road for the league and even for Article X. "The great purpose of the league is to make peace permanent and avoid war where that is humanly possible. The whole world is waiting to hear from the Senate." The press, however, was now more critical of Taft's actions and motives. "Possibly the physique of former President Taft accounts for his floundering so hopelessly," observed the *Fort Wayne News and Sentinel*. The Hays letters, wrote the *Miami Herald*, "contained a suggestion that Mr. Taft was carrying water on both shoulders."[3]

The limits of Taft's influence on the Senate debate became evident when Senator Henry Cabot Lodge delivered his first major speech after the president's return from Europe. Lodge and Taft had never been close in Republican politics. The Massachusetts senator had reservations about Taft's skills as a leader and in 1916 expressed "great doubts about the soundness of anything of which Taft was the head."[4] They had contended for the esteem of Theodore Roosevelt. Lodge had a head start there since his friendship with the president dated back to the mid-1880s. During the years of Roosevelt's presidency, however, Lodge had moved away from his old friend on issues of reform and regulation. Taft had remained loyal and, of course, became the heir apparent in 1908.

Lodge later claimed in 1912 that he had "been trying for three years" to support Taft's administration. In private letters to Roosevelt, he had observed that "the one thing which surprises me about Taft is that he does not know more about politics." A few months later, Lodge told Roosevelt that Taft "fails to interest the country." The Massachusetts senator supported Taft over Roosevelt in 1912 because "Taft stands for representative government and the maintenance of the independence of the courts." Lodge's divergence from Roosevelt came at some cost to their friendship; Edith Roosevelt never forgave his apostasy. In spite of his support of Taft, Lodge had no inherent regard for him as either a man or a politician.[5]

The former president and the senator also encountered tension in the tangled Republican politics of Massachusetts. Mabel Boardman's sister was the wife of Winthrop Murray Crane, who had been Lodge's Senate colleague. Crane believed in the League of Nations with an intensity even stronger than Taft's. Moreover, in Massachusetts the discreet and silent Crane often wielded more influence than did the aloof and cold Lodge. The distance between Taft and Lodge surfaced in the letter that Taft wrote the senator to congratulate him on his moving eulogy to Roosevelt in the Senate. Addressed to "My dear Senator Lodge," the letter read, "I think I knew Roosevelt as few knew him, except yourself, Root and two or three others, and I therefore feel competent to express an opinion of your picture of him." Taft lavished praise on the senator's words, but Lodge may well have thought that the former president did not deserve to be mentioned as Roosevelt's friend in the same manner as Lodge himself.[6]

Lodge's attack on the league as a return of the Holy Alliance of the nineteenth century drew headlines. His insistence on reservations about Article X emphasized Lodge's differences with the president and reflected the Republican consensus around major changes in the pact before it could be approved. The press did not observe that the speech also assailed as ineffective the major suggestions about reservations that Taft had proposed three weeks earlier. Lodge in effect sent the former president a signal that his overtures to Republican senators through the Hays letters had failed.[7]

Taft responded with a lengthy newspaper column that addressed Lodge's main points. Speaking of Lodge's general approach, Taft argued that "neither he nor any other opponent of the League seems to regard the Treaty of Peace as something to be executed. Its chief function now is to furnish objects of critical attack." Taft made some salient points about the limits of Lodge's intellectual assessment of the peace treaty. However, by the time he articulated these caveats, Taft had abandoned the position of unconditional ratification of the treaty that he and the League to Enforce Peace had once occupied. Lodge had been correct when he said of the Hays letters and Taft's position "the main thing is that he is accepting reservations, which is all the country will care to know. It is a sign of weakness."[8]

The course of the fight in the Senate over the League of Nations, and the president's response to his critics, soon overshadowed the controversy about Taft and the Hays letters. The Foreign Relations Committee had opened protracted hearings that stretched on into September. For his part, President Wilson had hardened his stance against any modifications in the treaty through Senate action. He had decided to take his case to the American people with a nation-wide tour in September. "Wilson is playing into their hands by his speeches in the West," Taft wrote of the president on the stump. He thought that "framing contemptuous phrases to characterize his opponents" was a grave error. By the end of September, Wilson had abandoned the remainder of his tour because of the poor health that had disabled him after a severe stroke in early October. Taft could see his dream of an organization devoted to world peace slipping away.[9]

Taft remained an oft-quoted public figure whose opinions on issues large and small attracted press attention. During his speaking tour, army aviators in Illinois invited the former president to go up in a plane. "I am not built for an airplane," replied Taft, whose weight now stood at 250 pounds. When railroad unions and their supporters advanced the Plumb Plan to nationalize the railroads, Taft opposed it as a form of communism. "We should not let the Soviet system gain even a toehold in America," he said in Cincinnati on 10 August 1919. Andrew Carnegie had died earlier in the year, and the release of his will brought news that he had left Taft a pension of $10,000 a year for life. After some initial reluctance, and at the urging of Nellie Taft, he decided to accept the bequest. With the winding up of the work of the National War Labor Board, Taft resumed his duties at Yale and closed up the apartment in Washington before returning to New Haven.[10]

Upon Wilson's return to Washington in late September, the lines had solidified on the league issue. Then came the news of the president's illness. The nation remained unaware of the extent of Wilson's disability, which rendered him incapable of full decision-making for weeks. Politicians grasped that ratification of the treaty would be with reservations or not at all. The president's reluctance to make any meaningful changes would ultimately defeat these compromise ideas, but Taft believed that he still might play a constructive role in such a process. He journeyed down to the capital to see if he might sway in a positive direction those regarded as mild reservationists, a bloc of seven to ten senators who could support reservations clarifying the meaning of the treaty, but did not wish to see the treaty itself defeated.

Controversy surrounded the Johnson amendment, named after its sponsor, Hiram Johnson of California, a leading irreconcilable. The proposal asserted that the United States should have as many votes in the internal workings of the league as did all the nations comprising the British Empire. Johnson's language reflected the anti-British views of many Americans that London and its several commonwealths would dominate the league to the disadvantage of the United States. Taft believed the Johnson amendment unneeded and unwise, and he went down to Washington in early October to rally support for its rejection.[11]

In addition to the mild reservationists, the other two main Republican blocs comprised the irreconcilables—such as William E. Borah and Hiram Johnson, who would not vote for the treaty under any circumstances—and a middle group. These senators under Lodge's direction sought tougher language in treaty reservations. Historians still disagree whether Lodge and his close allies ever wanted the treaty or were pursuing a strategy of obstruction and delay to encompass the ultimate rejection of the peace pact. The evidence indicates that Lodge hoped to see the treaty die. In Taft's case, he may well have suspected that Lodge was out to kill the treaty, but it would have amounted to political suicide for the former president to have uttered that thought in public.

Taft had good personal and political reasons for seeing Johnson's initiative fail. The California senator had been Theodore Roosevelt's running mate on the Progressive Party ticket in 1912 and had then made his way back to the Grand Old Party after 1913. Johnson had launched his presidential bid for 1920 and had taken to the hustings in search of delegates during the fall of 1919. Since everyone assumed that the Republicans were now more likely to win in 1920, the prospect of a Johnson presidency appalled Taft. In a speech in Indiana in September 1919, Johnson had derided Taft as "a distinguished ex-president who many respect but none follows." Of all the potential contenders for the White House, Johnson seemed unlikely to name Taft as chief justice should a vacancy occur with the death or retirement of Chief Justice Edward D. White.[12]

Taft's visit included testimony on 4 October before a House select committee to probe the possibility of creating a formal budget mechanism for the executive branch and Congress. Taft had made such proposals while president, but lawmakers had failed to act on them. So he gladly endorsed the concept of greater supervision of the government's spending practices: "I think the president ought to have the means of following the expenditures of the departments under appropriations." Taft and Secretary of the Treasury Carter Glass became the final witnesses before the panel.[13]

Once that obligation was discharged, Taft could turn to the even more important aspect of his Washington trip. He lobbied to defeat the Johnson amendment. He also sought reservations to the treaty that might enable the approval of the pact later in the fall. In one case, Taft's appeal led to a personal clash with a wavering senator. In a talk with Porter J. McCumber, a North Dakota Republican, and Frank B. Kellogg, another Republican lawmaker from Minnesota, the volatile Kellogg "said he wished the treaty was in hell." Taft asked him if he was for the treaty, "and he said he was." In the course of their exchange, Taft lost his temper. "Don't you know that you and these other conservatives are giving Johnson great help in his campaign for the Presidency?" Kellogg responded: "I know we are. Johnson is going to be nominated and elected President of the United States."

To this statement, Taft replied, with some heat: "Do you wish him to be president?" When Kellogg said, "No, of course not," Taft then commented, "Don't you propose to do what you can to prevent it?" Kellogg's reply that "we can not" led Taft to say, "You are just willing to make yourself a tail to his kite." After Kellogg said again that helping Johnson could not be avoided, Taft exploded:

"You haven't any guts to stand up and make the fight." Kellogg said he "would not take that from any man, and left the room." Taft wrote him a note of apology and good relations were restored. Nonetheless, Taft's skills as a negotiator on behalf of the treaty left much to be desired.[14]

Taft spoke with a number of mild reservationists and key Democrats during his days in Washington. The reporter for the *New-York Tribune*, a Republican paper opposed to both Wilson and the league, commented that "some irritation is being caused among the majority Republicans over the Taft conferences, but so far as reservations are concerned they are quite satisfied that Mr. Taft will not cause any change in the situation." Gus Karger, on the other hand, told Taft that "the general gossip here is to the effect that your visit has been productive of good and that it brought about a stiffening in the ranks of the mild reservationists. We shall see."[15]

Through the rest of October, Taft remained on the lecture circuit, speaking on behalf of ratification of the treaty. With Wilson sick and his ultimate fate uncertain, the anti-treaty forces gained momentum. During his Washington visit Taft had gone by the White House to pay his respects to the ailing president. Of course, he knew no more than the rest of the American people about Wilson's dire condition, since the president's doctors and wife kept a tight lid on any news about the gravity of his predicament. In fact, Wilson's stroke had rendered him unable to carry out his duties for a time and, more importantly for the treaty fight, had intensified his commitment to ratification without any reservations. These developments left Taft as the most public exponent of ratification, while at the same time a man without real influence to change Republican votes in Congress.

In mid-October a reporter encountered the former president in a Baltimore hotel. "Would you accept the nomination for President?" Taft responded with "a loud, hearty, and contagious laugh." To the waiting scribe, he said, "You are truly humorous." He emphasized that Democrats were the people uttering flattering remarks about him in the press. For his part, Taft wanted to "see the Republican party victorious everywhere."[16]

As Taft moved back toward the mainstream of the Republicans with his acceptance of treaty reservations, he also refurbished his conservative credentials with a harder line toward labor unrest and the threat of radicalism that he perceived behind the militancy. Speaking at a meeting in honor of Theodore Roosevelt on 26 October, Taft proclaimed that the "robust and triumphant Americanism" of Theodore Roosevelt would help to beat back the specter of "Bolshevism and extreme socialism" within the left wing of the labor movement. "We must resist this attempt to take the country by the throat and by a highwayman's method to force political and unreasonable economic concessions." The moderate and judicious Taft of the National War Labor Board had become a memory.[17]

Two days earlier the Senate had taken up the Johnson amendment that Taft so disliked, and in a surprise vote rejected it. This small procedural victory soon faded in importance as the lawmakers prepared to debate and vote on the treaty itself during November 1919. Taft wanted to see the long battle over the treaty come to an end. "The country is most impatient for ratification," he informed a close Senate ally. Taft probably misread the state of public opinion at this juncture. The efforts of the opponents of the treaty had undercut support for Wilson's vision, as worries about the effects of inflation, labor unrest, and social turmoil became uppermost among the average citizens. Wilson's intransigence and absence from the public debate left the Democrats and pro-league forces leaderless against Lodge and his allies.

Taft did his part to defeat the president at a meeting of the executive committee of the League to Enforce Peace on 13 November. After those present voted down a resolution against the Lodge reservations by a vote of ten against and five in favor, Taft spoke out in a most effective presentation. The chair of the group, A. Lawrence Lowell, said that "the opinion of this committee is that we had better accept the Treaty with such reservations as the majority pass rather than have it rejected by this present session of the Senate." Taft then urged that the action of his league's executive panel be communicated as soon as possible to Lodge and the Democratic leader, Gilbert M. Hitchcock of Nebraska. As John M. Cooper, the best student of the League of Nations fight, argues, the League to Enforce Peace responded in a predictable manner, given the crucial role of Taft in all its deliberations.[18]

For the public, the announcement on 18 November 1919 of the position of the League to Enforce Peace meant that Taft and the organization's leadership had identified themselves with the position of Lodge and the Republican senators. The influence of the League to Enforce Peace waned from this point, because of its criticism of the president and the Democrats while leaning toward Lodge and the Republicans. In effect, the group had sold out its principles and received nothing in return. The next day, the treaty went down to defeat when the Senate rejected the treaty with the Lodge reservations. Forty Democrats, acting at the direction of President Wilson, and the fifteen irreconcilables, cast votes against the Lodge version. A vote on unconditional ratification lost by a vote of fifty-three against and thirty-eight in favor.

Taft said in public, "I would rather have the treaty than nothing at all." In private, he assigned the blame for the outcome to both the president and Lodge. "The President is much at fault in this matter and so is Lodge. It is their personal vanity and partisanship which had led to this present situation." Taft had done his best to save the treaty throughout the League of Nations fight.

He had, however, occupied an impossible position. The Republicans were never going to accept a treaty that Woodrow Wilson negotiated without serious changes. Wilson's distrust of the opposition and his faith in his own abilities meant that he was reluctant to conciliate Lodge and other GOP senators. Taft sought a middle ground that did not exist. If Taft proposed changes that the president accepted, the Republicans felt emboldened to ask for more. When Taft failed to deliver Republican votes after Wilson made concessions, then the White House felt betrayed and lost all confidence in the former president. Had Taft simply been an honest broker with no agenda of his own, his mediation efforts might have had a better chance. But when it came right down to the Republican Party or the League of Nations as Republicans wanted it, Taft had no serious option. Wilson and the League of Nations could not make William Howard Taft the next Chief Justice of the United States. Only a Republican president, elected in 1920, could do that. Taft was not going to shatter his life's ambition with a sacrificial gesture toward Woodrow Wilson, whom at bottom he despised.

Like many pro-league advocates, Taft did not believe in November 1919 that the Senate rejection of the treaty should end the matter. He hoped that, after a suitable interval of reflection, the lawmakers might be persuaded to rethink their votes and put the treaty through. The maneuvering had already begun for the 1920 presidential election. The race for the Republican nomination would further complicate an already confused parliamentary situation in the Senate. As January 1920 moved toward February, Taft wailed to a correspondent: "Oh Lord, how long are they going to delay in Washington?"[19]

Until Theodore Roosevelt's death in January 1919, Republican leaders assumed that the former president stood as the presumptive nominee in 1920. With Roosevelt removed, the field of hopefuls lacked a strong front-runner. As Taft's remarks in October 1919 indicated, the conservative wing of the party had little regard for Hiram Johnson as a potential standard-bearer for the party. As 1920 began, the more obvious leaders included General Leonard Wood, the political heir of Roosevelt, and Governor Frank O. Lowden of Illinois. Taft did not have a great admiration for Wood, whom he regarded as having the faults of Roosevelt without many of his virtues. "Wood has a lot of amateurs," Taft wrote, "and his turning from one supporter and then another makes the boys feel that possibly they are not going to be solid with him when they deliver the goods."[20]

Lowden had the advantages of a Midwestern base and access to the fortune of the Pullman railroad car through his wife. He had come out for the treaty with the Lodge reservations, which pleased Taft at this point: "I would like to have Lowden nominated, if we cannot do better, because he has made a firm declaration about the League, and because I think he is more amenable to reason than any of those prominently named." Lowden had corresponding weaknesses. The money that he spread around from his war chest funded some shady delegate arrangements, especially in Missouri.[21]

In a survey of Republican candidates that he wrote for his column in early January, Taft added Warren G. Harding to the field of front-runners along with Wood and Lowden. As a fellow Ohioan, Harding represented a familiar political commodity to the former president. He had supported Taft in 1912 and had delivered an effective keynote address at the Republican convention in 1916. The senator's extramarital relationship with a woman in his hometown of Marion, Ohio, did not enter into Taft's appraisal of his presidential hopes. "Senator Harding has a taking personality, is a handsome man and a graceful forcible speaker," Taft wrote. Based on nothing but his intuition, Taft concluded that Harding "would be glad to have the Treaty and the League ratified with compromise reservations, and will finally vote to that end." Taft would spend most of 1920 convincing himself that Harding was a League supporter at heart, in the face of overwhelming evidence in the opposite direction.[22]

Taft saw the election as a referendum on Wilson and his record of eight years in office. He deplored "the partisan conduct of the war and the partisan making of the peace, against extravagance and unnecessary taxation, against the ruthless exercise of one-man power in passing on important national policies and carrying them out." These criticisms would provide the key to Republican victory. As for Wilson himself, "my contempt for him is deeply embedded."[23]

The events following the defeat of the treaty in the Senate had intensified Taft's visceral dislike of the president. Like many moderate Republicans, Taft had hoped that public sentiment in favor of the pact might lead the Republicans in the Senate to reconsider what they had done in November 1919. The sober second thought of the nation, Taft believed, would grasp the underlying good points of the treaty and demand Senate approval. For Wilson, however, ill and out of touch in his White House sickroom, the treaty as he had brought it back from Paris with Article X intact represented the only acceptable outcome of the struggle with the upper house.

During December 1919, Taft spoke out for compromise and re-visiting the negative vote on the treaty. He assigned most of the blame for the defeat to Wilson, with some residual criticism of Lodge. On 23 November, a meeting of the executive committee of the League to Enforce Peace, at which Taft presided, called on the eighty members of the Senate who had voted for the League of Nations in some form to act. "The fate of the treaty rests in their hands. They have the votes. They have the power. Theirs is the responsibility. They must get together." A week later, speaking in Springfield, Massachusetts, Taft observed, "I would rather have the treaty with reservations than nothing at all."[24]

By all accounts, the vagaries of public opinion had little effect on the Senate during the last weeks of 1919. Individual senators, supporters to some degree of the treaty in one form or another, came together to discuss possible ways to see the pact through the ratification process. Woodrow Wilson did not make their task any easier. In mid-December, for example, he issued a public statement that as president "he has no compromise or concession of any kind in mind, but intends, so far as he is concerned, that the Republican leaders of the Senate shall continue to bear the undivided respon-sibility for the fate of the treaty and the present condition of the world in consequence of that fate." For Taft these words embodied nothing more than face-saving and political machinations on the part of the president.[25]

At the end of December, friends of the League of Nations pro-posed that Taft speak to a non-partisan meeting in Washington on behalf of the league and its ratification. When asked for his opin-ion on this idea, Senator Borah retorted, "I don't very well see how I could say anything about a political mummy." The proposed speech did not occur, and Taft did not return to Washington for three weeks. He was still speaking out in favor of a compromise, but by the time he did so in the nation's capital the prospects for a bipartisan settlement of the league issue had collapsed.[26]

Beginning soon after the November defeat of the treaty, mild res-ervationists launched an effort to find common ground with the Democrats. The lawmakers learned over the holidays from their constituents that sentiment existed in the country to have the treaty ratified and the uncertainty of the political and economic situation put to rest. When Congress reconvened for its regular session in December 1919, serious talks began among groups of senators to find a way to get the treaty approved in a manner that moderates from both parties could endorse. By mid-January, Senator Charles McNary of Oregon informed Taft that he had hopes for a settlement even though "the trouble in the situation is that the President treats the Covenant as sacred, and Mr. Lodge treats the reservations as sacred." Taft told Gus Karger on 21 January: "The only way that Lodge can be brought around is to put him in a minority in the Senate, and if enough mild reservationists could unite with the Democrats and do that, even though it does not mean two thirds, it will put him where he belongs and where he does not like to appear."[27]

The bipartisan accord, which to some senators seemed close on 22 January, fell apart the very next day. The irreconcilables learned what was going on and threatened Lodge with a revolt, including his ouster as Majority Leader, if he persisted in discussions with the Democrats and the mild reservationists. Faced with the threat of losing his leadership post, Lodge backed down. He told the Democrats that there could be no changes from the reservations on Article X and the Monroe Doctrine as worked out in November. The prospect of a compromise agreement, never very realistic, was dead. Taft visited the Senate on 23 January, but he had little impact on the proceedings. "The matter of ratification of the treaty is in the hands of the senators. It must be worked out by them."[28]

In the week that followed, Taft made one more attempt to work out a viable compromise. He sketched a version of a reservation to Article X that he hoped would satisfy his Republican friends. Extensive debate had occurred over whether Article X—which pledged the United States to preserve the territorial integrity and independence of member states against external aggression—represented a legal obligation or a moral obligation. Wilson had said no legal obligation existed but that a moral obligation to intervene represented a higher value. Taft's proposed reservation denied that his country would assume any "legal or binding obligation" to enforce Article X at all, but that Congress would consider the extent to which the United States might "in the interest of world peace and justice" find a moral obligation to intervene.[29]

When the Democrats put forward Taft's idea on 30 January, Lodge turned the proposal down flat. He would not countenance the former president's wording, and instead stood by the reservation about Article X that was part of his package of reservations. This exchange led to a final breakdown of the talks on a compromise proposal regarding the league. The pact would be taken up in the Senate in February and March, but the prospects for its approval were slim unless one side or the other shifted its position.

The day after his draft reservation on Article X was rejected, Taft thought that a new development might change the minds of some of the senators and perhaps even that of the president. On 31 January the former foreign minister of Great Britain, Edward Grey (now Viscount Grey), published a letter in one of his country's newspapers in which he recommended that his government accept the Lodge reservations as the price for getting the United States to enter the league. Grey's words undermined Wilson's argument that any change in the language of the treaty would require renegotiating the whole document. The Republicans made much of Grey's statements, and Taft thought for a brief moment that ratification was ensured. "I am hopeful," he wrote on 6 February 1920, "however, that Lord Grey's letter has cleared up the situation, and that ratification is likely to come—ungraciously—but to come."[30]

Taft believed at this point that "the League is defective" and would need much tinkering and many changes to make it work for peace. American participation was essential. Getting the United States "inside the door" would be the "great triumph." Once a partner in the operations of the League of Nations, "all this bother through which we have been and all this bitterness of discussion we may well forget in the real step forward that has been taken in bringing the nations to the council table permanently for consideration of every issue arising." Assuming eventual ratification as he did, Taft contended the debate over the League "was of great educational effect through the country and roused the public opinion of those who ultimately constitute the conscience of the country in reference to our obligations in the world. This is a great advance."[31]

The Grey letter proved to be only a passing moment in the continued deadlock between the president and Lodge over the fate of the treaty. Outraged at what Grey had said, the president chose this opportunity to rid himself of his secretary of state, Robert Lansing. Arguing that Lansing had been convening Cabinet meetings while Wilson was ill, Wilson sent a tart letter asking the secretary for an explanation of these alleged actions. The outcome was Lansing's resignation, along with much embarrassment for the president, who now appeared to be petty, small, and vindictive. The press asked Taft for his opinion. "I believe that Secretary Lansing was acting altogether within his rights in calling conferences of cabinet members. I would not call them cabinet meetings." Taft predicted that the public would agree with the secretary of state.[32]

In his columns for the *Philadelphia Public Ledger*, Taft gave the Grey letter ample attention as part of a potential settlement of the league controversy. In fact, by February 1920, the prospects for a compromise resolution of the league issue were dimming. The contestants in the Senate had taken up strong positions. Unless Wilson expressed a desire for compromise, a break in the stalemate could not happen. Wilson had not overcome the effects of his stroke, and his health worsened again during this period. He even entertained the delusion that he might gain the Democratic nomination for a third term. Taft exclaimed on 22 February 1920, "I am bitterly disappointed with the whole Senate—Democrats, Republicans and mild reservationists. They seem to fiddle while Rome is burning. I fear that Wilson's outrageous conduct toward Lansing has stiffened the Republicans against any compromise." Meanwhile, the Democrats sought to make the league a 1920 campaign issue. Thinking that the basic differences among the senators came down to only "the form of words," Taft told his editor at the *Public Ledger*, "I can not restrain my profanity."[33]

Taft had ample reason to indulge his capacity for swearing over the next month as the drama in the Senate played out to its now inevitable conclusion. On 19 March the lawmakers took their final votes and the treaty failed for the last time. The pact with the Lodge reservations fell seven votes short of approval. Wilson had instructed the Democrats not to support this option. Their votes along with those of the irreconcilables doomed the treaty. Taft knew where he would put the blame. "The President has destroyed the Treaty he made, and he has destroyed himself, so far as the issue on the Treaty is concerned. He has made the position of the Democracy even more hopeless than it was." Taft was ready to take to the hustings against Wilson and to make speeches, as he put it, *"con amore."*[34]

Working out just what role Taft might play in the Republican campaign presented practical difficulties. While there were voices here and there that talked of him as a presidential candidate, Taft maintained the same posture of amusement in public on that subject he had adopted since leaving the White House. Amid the furor over the bipartisan compromise talks in January 1920, he had told reporters: "I am not an aspirant for the Presidential nomination. I will in no way seek the nomination, and the sooner my friends get the idea out of their heads the better."[35]

Taft did not even plan to attend the national convention. If he went, he would go as a delegate from New Haven among the Republican contingent from Connecticut. As he told his editor in Philadelphia, "For various reasons I have made arrangements which will prevent my being there. I expect to be engaged in a speaking tour at that time."[36] Taft also had impending personal and professional commitments that were going to occupy his time during the spring and summer of 1920.

Taft's daughter Helen had been pursuing an academic career during her father's postpresidential phase. After undergraduate years at Bryn Mawr College, she did graduate work in history at Yale University. Returning to Bryn Mawr to teach, she became the dean of the college at the age of twenty-six, and served as acting president in the absence of the president, M. Carey Thomas. Amid this busy schedule, she had fallen in love with another graduate student,

Frederick J. Manning, when they shared a seminar at Yale. The couple decided early in 1920 to get married.[37]

The prospective bride's father had mixed feelings about the imminent nuptials. He wanted his daughter to complete her graduate work and in time obtain a doctorate in history. Accordingly, he feared that "your marriage will probably end that career, if your married life is as happy as I hope it may be." Frederick Manning was younger than his bride, and so Taft worried his daughter might be "unconsciously stimulated in your enthusiasm for this marriage by the thought that you are approaching thirty and yearn for the happiness of family life. You are a woman of poise and level headed and I can not think this." Notwithstanding the implicit reservations of her father, Helen Taft knew her own mind, and she and Manning were married on 15 July 1920 at Murray Bay with the family in attendance. Their union proved a happy one.[38]

In his legal affairs, Taft assumed a large commitment during the spring of 1920 that would keep him traveling in Canada for the next year. The Grand Trunk Railway system, a private corporation, had encountered financial difficulty and the Canadian government was in the process of taking it over. The issue then arose of the value of the common and preferred stock of the corporation, and the extent to which it had any monetary value. The government in Ottawa created a Grand Trunk Arbitration Board, consisting of three members. The Grand Trunk line would have the opportunity to pick a representative, and by June 1920 Taft was in negotiations about the position.[39]

As some Canadians pointed out, Taft's presence reflected a certain irony in action of the Canadian government. Nine years earlier during Taft's presidency, the Conservative Party had opposed the proposed reciprocal trade agreement that the White House and the Liberal government of Wilfred Laurier had worked out. The allegation had been that Taft wanted to make Canada an economic satellite of the United States. The rejection of reciprocity by Canadian voters in September 1911 had been one of the most bitter defeats that Taft had experienced in office. A friend of Taft and fellow resident of Murray Bay, Rodolphe Lemieux, a former postmaster general in the Liberal government, told reporters, "Time brings its revenges and this only caps a long series of events which shows that we were right in 1911."[40]

Taft would need to spend extended periods in Canada inspecting the physical plant and financial records of the Grand Trunk line. He would have his vacation in Murray Bay, especially with Helen Taft Manning's wedding, and so campaigning for the Republican presidential candidate would be a limited part of Taft's hectic agenda in the last nine months of 1920.

In early June, after a tumultuous national convention, the Republicans selected Warren G. Harding as their standard-bearer against the Democrats. Taft had wired the Republican nominee at once to say, "I congratulate you most sincerely on your election. I am confident of your election and predict for you a most useful and successful administration." In a similar missive to Harding's running mate, Governor Calvin Coolidge of Massachusetts, Taft predicted: "The ticket of Harding and Coolidge should sweep the country."[41]

Taft's reading of the political portents was correct. After eight years of Democratic rule, the American people had had enough of Woodrow Wilson and his policies. The high cost of living, the strikes and racial unrest, the sense that government had become too big and intrusive, and the alienation of key Democratic voting blocs such as the Irish over the rejection of the treaty, all these elements made for a Republican year. Henry Cabot Lodge had sounded the Republican themes in his keynote address. He emphasized the alleged lack of legitimacy embodied in Democratic rule. "Mr. Wilson stands for a theory of administration and government which is not American."[42]

In such an environment, Harding was likely to prosper with Republicans. Hiram Johnson called him "a suave, pleasant personality without an atom of principle." Taft was closer to the mark with his assessment. Harding was "a regular Republican, believing in the necessity and efficacy of solid party action as the only effective means of interpreting the will of the people into constructive progress." But for Taft the larger issue in the Harding candidacy became where the nominee stood on American entry into the League of Nations. If Harding could be persuaded to support the treaty with the Lodge reservations, win the election, and then put Taft on the Supreme Court, the eight years that the former president had spent in the political wilderness would not have been empty ones. He would have achieved the twin aspects of his heart's desire, a major step forward toward world peace and the judicial appointment he wanted more than anything in the world. The campaign of 1920 would determine whether that happy result could be attained.[43]

8

AMBITION ACHIEVED:
CHIEF JUSTICE TAFT

There was never any doubt that William Howard Taft would support the Republican presidential ticket in 1920. The Democrats had nominated an Ohioan, Governor James M. Cox, and selected Franklin Delano Roosevelt of New York as his running mate. Even though Cox and Roosevelt endorsed the League of Nations as Woodrow Wilson had conceived it, Taft was not about to bolt for a Democrat and end any chances of the Supreme Court in his future. In addition, he had little respect for Cox, who had a tangled and tawdry marital history in Ohio. As he put it in late September, "Cox, as a presidential possibility, is not a very big figure. He is showing himself a pretty small ward politician."[1]

The central question for Taft involved aligning his own position on the League of Nations with that of the Republican nominee. If Warren G. Harding had rejected the Treaty of Versailles outright, Taft would have faced a difficult public choice. Supporting an irreconcilable senator as the GOP nominee would at the very least have been most embarrassing. At worst the former president would have looked like someone who had sold out his principles for partisan reasons. As he argued in somewhat lame fashion, "Those who are supporting Mr. Harding on the faith of his seeking a modified League will do the best that can be done for the cause of a League."[2]

Where did Warren G. Harding stand on the issue of the League of Nations? His first extended discussion of his approach to the treaty and its ratification had come on 11 September 1919, when he led off the Senate debate for the Republicans. Harding's prose resembled a senatorial squid, squirting gobs of sonorous rhetoric at the contested issues. Oozing ponderous paragraphs, Harding revealed disdain for President Wilson and the offshoot of his diplomatic efforts in Paris. Harding called it his "deliberate conviction that the league of nations covenant, as negotiated at Paris and signed at Versailles, either creates a super-government of the nations which enter it or it will prove the colossal disappointment of the ages." The Ohio senator "could not believe this Republic ought to sanction it in either case."[3]

After attacking Wilson on several aspects of the treaty and asserting the superior claims of American nationalism, Harding concluded: "I do not see how any Senator can decide upon his final vote till the disputed amendments and proposed reservations shall have the stamp of the decision of a Senate majority. I can never cast a vote to ratify without safeguards." For Harding, serious changes had to come from the Senate in the autumn of 1919. "We know now there are to be reservations, unmistakable reservations, else there will be no treaty." And the reservations must be tough, he added. "I could no more support 'mild reservations' than I could support mild Americanism."[4]

For a man who had been in politics as long as Taft, he had the odd habit of taking what his fellow Republicans said as valid on its face as long as it suited his current point of view. A wily operator such as Harding, untethered to honesty and with an eye on the White House, could frame his language to convey the opposite meaning of what he really believed without quite lying. For example, he adopted a posture of seeming to be open-minded about the League of Nations during the first half of 1919, when he really was just waiting until the senatorial opposition gained followers. "We have the strength to defeat the plans of President Wilson in foisting upon us his interwoven league of nations," he said in private. At bottom he believed that "I do not think the Senate is ever going to consent to ratify the League of Nations Covenant which subjects us either to Great Britain or to a super-government of the world."[5] How Harding got these dire options out of the league that Wilson had framed he never explained. His opinions, however, echoed what his fellow lawmakers said in and out of the cloakroom.

Once nominated as a compromise choice for the Republicans in June 1920, Harding sought party unity on the league issue above all other considerations. Like most other Republicans, he believed that the election should produce a Republican triumph because of the mounting public disgust with Wilson and the Democrats. The only hope for Cox and Roosevelt lay in a split within the Grand Old Party over the league and internationalism. Harding wanted to play down differences, conciliate both sides, and let time pass until the voters went to the polls. He could stand on the platform of the convention, an empty document that Elihu Root had framed, which said very little specifically about the League of Nations. It endorsed an international association but one that "must be based on international justice," whatever that meant.[6]

Taft could have divined Harding's ultimate position from the choices the candidate made about which Republican faction to address first. The nominee sought to get Hiram Johnson on board at the start, and managed that feat through the use of adroit language in his acceptance speech. The Republican platform itself had been constructed to keep Johnson in the fold with its vague language and its failure to mention the league at all. That sent a clear message to Johnson. There would be in the Harding presidency "no surrender of rights to a world council, or its military alliance, no assumed mandatory, however appealing, ever shall summon the sons of this republic to war." Johnson praised what the candidate had said as being in line with his own views of the league and the problems it posed. The California senator expressed confidence that, in his words, President Harding would "scrap the Wilson League of Nations."[7]

In the face of Harding's deference to Hiram Johnson, it took a great deal of hard swallowing for Taft to endorse the nominee's position on the league. As Taft noted in his newspaper column in early August, "Senator Harding's speech of acceptance was disappointing to many loyal Republicans because of his failure to say that when he became President he would consistently put through the League of Nations with the reservations for which thirty-four Republican senators, including himself and Senator Lodge, within a year have voted twice." Taft noted that "the weight of emphasis he uses in his condemnation of the League" was glaring in the absence of its outright endorsement of the league with reservations.[8]

Had Taft drawn the logical conclusion that Harding opposed the league and was unlikely to proceed to its ratification upon becoming president, he would then have been faced with the choice of bolting the party or choking down a foreign policy of which he disapproved. Knowing that his only chance to be chief justice (assuming the retirement or death of Chief Justice White) hung in the balance too, Taft set about finding a way to rationalize support for Harding and his party on grounds other than the league fight.

When he did that, he found ample reasons to vote Republican. Writing again in the friendly confines of the *Yale Review*, Taft acknowledged the president's enfeebled physical condition and then launched into an extended indictment of his eight-year record. He found Wilson's lack of consultation, especially with Republicans during the war, very troubling. The war, Taft argued, was won in spite of Wilson's executive style. The president was influenced by pacifists, delayed the full implementation of the draft, and sought a negotiated peace. Taft based these judgments on what he believed was credible information, though that inside data often diverged from the facts. Any fellow feeling for Wilson's situation as president, based on his own experience in the White House, had long since left Taft's mind.

In domestic affairs, Taft alleged, Wilson had "appointed many persons of socialistic tendency to office and power." He was too deferential to labor unions and "largely influenced" by Samuel Gompers. Above all, "the people are tired of his autocratic methods of government, whether necessary for war or not, and they are disposed to end them by a change of party control." Harding, on the other hand, "is a regular Republican and is conservative in his tendency, though not reactionary."[9]

Making a partisan Republican case for Harding gave Taft no difficulty. Squaring the circle about his candidate's stance on the

League of Nations was another proposition entirely. His correspondents asked him how he could reconcile his opinions on the league with what the Republican presidential candidate advocated on the stump. His answer reflected the partisan choice he had made to vote for Harding. "I am very much disappointed, as you are, in respect to Senator Harding's position, but I think he may be brought to accept the solution which we would have after all. I think he is going to be elected and I think we must vote for him."[10]

Two days after writing this letter, Taft could have read in the *Washington Post* an article based on leaks from the Harding camp in which it was stated that "the hope publicly expressed by former President Taft that Senator Harding will stand for the Wilson League of Nations is doomed to disappointment." If elected, the story went on, Harding had no intention of submitting the Treaty of Versailles, even with the crippling Lodge reservations, to the Senate. Instead, he intended to start over on the basis of language from Elihu Root and others to create "an association of nations" that would evolve in the course of his administration once elected. The vagueness of the proposal and the empty language could not disguise the essential message that Taft's belief about Harding's eventual endorsement of the league was a non-starter.[11]

The *New York World*, a pro-Wilson Democratic newspaper, had asked Taft to respond to their pointed questions about the league, and he did so in a letter that appeared on 6 August. The editors of the paper asked him whether Harding's proposal for an association of nations to create "a new relationship of the nations to commit the moral forces of the world to peace and justice" could be more practical than "the concrete present, actual existence and availability of a League that twenty-nine nations have already joined?"[12]

Taft believed that Harding's proposal would be unacceptable among the twenty-nine members of the existing League. As a result, the new president "will ultimately consider it to be wiser to enter the league with the Lodge reservations than to attempt to carry out the same purpose through a new form of association." Taft based this claim on nothing more than a fond hope that the future president would come around to his way of thinking. The

Taft and Harding. President Harding and Chief Justice Taft share a smile at the White House. (Library of Congress LC-DIG-hec-30877)

headline in the *New York Times* read, "Taft Clashes with Harding on League," which was something more than the exchange with the *World* indicated.[13]

In a highly personal column for the *Philadelphia Ledger*, Taft sought to explain his position to people who asked him if he wanted the league so much, why did he not vote for James Cox? While he regarded Harding's approach of starting all over with a new association of nations as "unwise, politically inexpedient, and impractical," Taft expected that the new president, assuming a Harding victory, would come back to the league with the Lodge reservations. Cox, on the other hand, would present the Wilsonian league to a Republican minority in the Senate still able to block ratification of the treaty in the unlikely event of a Democratic triumph in the fall. Taft had no intention of deserting his party to pursue a course that Cox would hardly be able to achieve in the improbable event of his winning the election.[14]

Having decided on his path in the fall election, Taft prepared to go forward and speak for Harding on the stump, following his vacation and his work on the Grand Trunk Railway. In the meantime, he advised the leadership of the League to Enforce Peace that if it moved off its position of endorsing ratification of the treaty with the Lodge reservations, he would resign as president of the organization. From such a perspective, he argued that it was "greatly better" for the league to "remain quiet and use such influence as it has after the election. Were it to go against this advice, he would step down with the inevitable public furor and the probable demise of the League to Enforce Peace itself.[15] So much for the bright hopes that Taft had once invested in his league as a means of achieving world peace.

Throughout August, Taft continued to tell friends and correspondents that he hoped Harding would come out for ultimate ratification of the treaty as amended. "I am hopeful that Harding may acquire some wiser environment than he now seems to have and may give to the friends of the League hope of that which they have a right to expect from him in the way of a League with reservations." Why Taft believed that Harding would abandon the position he had developed with such tenacity and consistency during 1919 and 1920 remains mysterious. Toward the middle of August 1920 he could only advance the lame argument that "we have just as much chance of getting to the League with reservations through Harding as with Cox—indeed I think a little more."[16]

As the fall campaign opened, the Democrats wanted to keep the focus on the League of Nations issue. With their canvass in difficulty and the public tired of Wilson, splitting the Republicans between those who followed Taft and those who supported Hiram Johnson and William E. Borah seemed the best hope for the Democratic cause. The Republicans, on the other hand, wanted to base their appeal on the animosity toward Wilson. As Will Hays put it, the majority of Americans believed the Democrats stood for "a saturnalia of extravagance, a cataclysm of perverted purposes and broken promises, and, finally, an absolute betrayal of American rights and American interests."[17]

One of the major complaints of Taft and other critics of Wilson about the league (and his entire presidency) was the alleged lack of consultation throughout the administration. In his *Yale Review* essay, Taft cited many instances when the president should have consulted with the political opposition. The theme of one-man rule became a favorite Republican refrain. The members of the Grand Old Party did not add that their cooperation would have rested on Wilson adopting their policies while they reserved the right to assail the president as a dictator anyway.

To the president's secretary, Joseph P. Tumulty, and others in the White House, the opportunity proved too tempting to miss. When James M. Cox asked them in late September "if I might have your permission to use cable messages passing between yourself and Judge Taft showing your acceptance of his proposals," the president authorized their release to the Democratic presidential candidate. While not "particularly keen about having it exploited because I am ashamed to have taken the advice of those insincere men who are not trying to help but trying to embarrass and to hinder," Wilson thought that the documents Tumulty possessed contained "the germs of many fine campaign speeches."[18]

Two weeks later, the Cox campaign released the documents that the White House had furnished to them. The cablegrams had been sent in March and April of 1919, when Taft had asked Tumulty if he might send Wilson some suggestions for revisions in the proposed Treaty of Versailles that might help secure ratification. Cox asserted that Taft's advice was "not only found most helpful in the formation of the covenant, but it was followed." He went on to say that Taft had committed himself in a moral way to the league but had now taken an "equivocal position in supporting Harding." The documents, Cox added, came from a time when Taft's "sincerity of mind and intelligence were not beclouded by the partisan prejudice of a political campaign."[19]

Taft responded to the Cox disclosures with public calm. He said he had told "an emissary of the White House" to publish the documents. "I had frequently referred to the correspondence myself and would probably have published it, had it been my business to do so." Gus Karger looked into the matter and concluded that Taft thought the reporter acted as the "emissary," but Karger had not served in that role. The White House, Karger believed, "acted without information as to your own wishes and was driven to the publication, without authority, by the desperate condition of the campaign."[20] In another letter to the former president, Karger observed four days later: "If Jim Cox isn't riding to one of the most disastrous defeats ever experienced by a Democratic candidate, ninety percent of the American people are off in their political prognostications.[21]

Taft had now finished his Grand Trunk work and was prepared to devote the last two weeks of October to the Republican campaign. He wired his secretary, Wendell Mischler, "I need you badly in my campaign" as he prepared to depart for Michigan and upstate New York. He did so in the wake of a statement from Harding in Des Moines, Iowa, where he seemed to reject the League of Nations and reservations altogether: "I do not want to clarify these obligations. I want to turn my back on them." He went on to say that "the proposed league strikes a deadly blow at our constitutional integrity and surrenders to a dangerous extent our independence of action." Finally, he repeated that he would, as a new president, pursue an "association of nations."[22]

As he had before, Taft proceeded to accept Harding's words as a restatement of the candidate's position on the league or an association of nations rather than a rejection of the concept as a policy proposal. On the road, he fired off letters to skeptical correspondents asserting that "the only hope of the League of Nations is through the election of Mr. Harding." In his prepared remarks, he denied that Harding would "scrap" the league but would rather renegotiate the pact with "the leading powers now in the League" before sending the revised treaty to the Senate. He alleged that Wilson had "jealousy of power" and believed in a "personal system of government." These elements had led the president to destroy "his own brainchild of the League of Nations."[23]

By this point in the campaign, Taft had determined to support

Republicans all along the line. In his own state of Connecticut, the incumbent senator, Frank Brandegee, was in a tough race with a Democratic challenger. An irascible alcoholic and an irreconcilable of the most intense and vituperative sort, Brandegee faced Augustine Lonergan, a member of the House who favored the league. Taft received a letter from Richard Hooker, the editor of the *Springfield Republican*, an influential GOP newspaper in western Massachusetts. In it, Hooker cited Brandegee's unpleasant personal qualities. He also noted the recent death of Murray Crane, a mutual friend of both Hooker and Taft.

At the Republican National Convention, the ailing Crane, a passionate advocate of the League of Nations, had endeavored to have the party platform endorse the Treaty of Versailles with the Lodge reservations. In the course of intense discussions about the question, Brandegee had cursed Crane in the most abusive terms. For Hooker the Connecticut senator's actions meant he could not endorse the incumbent's reelection. Another problem was Brandegee's scornful references to women's suffrage. Hooker hoped that Taft would decide not to vote for Brandegee in light of these compelling reasons.[24]

Taft answered that his personal, negative feelings about Brandegee had not entered into his decision to vote for the Republican senator. He returned to blaming Wilson for the debacle over the league, and thus saw Harding as the only hope for a positive result. If Brandegee in the Senate would make life easier for a President Harding, then he deserved support, notwithstanding his treatment of their mutual friend, Murray Crane. "But I must stand by my own reasoning and own judgment," Taft replied, "even though it brings down on my head charges of inconsistency, which I don't recognize the justice of."[25]

Whatever Taft's course in the election had been, he received welcome news on election night. Harding and the Republicans swamped the Democrats in one of the greatest election triumphs in the nation's history. Harding gathered more than sixteen million votes to Cox's eight million plus ballots. The Republicans had 404 electoral votes to 127 for the Democrats. In the Senate, in a result that particularly concerned Taft, the Republicans would enjoy a 59 to 37 margin. That meant, for the former president, that mavericks such as Johnson, Borah, and La Follette would not be able to frustrate Harding. This assumed, however, that Harding would behave toward the League in a manner that these irreconcilables could not support.

"I congratulate you, the Nation and the World on your triumphant election," Taft wired Harding as the results made clear the extent of the Republican victory. He praised "the dignity, courtesy, sense of responsibility and self-restraint with which you carried yourself in the election under the greatest provocation to a different course, must in my judgment afford great satisfaction to yourself, as they do to your supporters."[26]

Taft referred to the charges made late in the campaign that Harding had African-American ancestors. He had heard about the allegations leveled against Harding and he wanted the Harding leadership to be prepared to meet them. The controversy did not affect the outcome of the election, though the whispering tactic against Harding had some staying power in the South.[27]

Harding replied that he hoped Taft would come to Marion, Ohio, in mid-December. "I very much wish to confer with you on our place in international relations, and get your views as to the best proposal on which we may hope to unite American sentiment." The meeting did not in fact occur until Christmas Eve, but Taft naturally tried to anticipate which subjects might arise, including a possible appointment to the Supreme Court. Newspaper speculation to that effect had started soon after the votes were counted. On 8 November, the *Washington Times* carried a story, "Predict Taft Will Be Chief Justice," that said Chief Justice Edward D. White had prepared to retire and Taft would likely be his successor.[28]

While he waited for his meeting with Harding, Taft continued to speak out on public matters. He took a strong position against the endemic anti-Semitism of the postwar period. During his negotiations with Wilson in 1919, he had urged the president to have the league covenant include a statement on religious freedom. He feared that if such language vanished, the Jews in the United States would oppose the league. Several months later in a speech to the National Geographic Society, the former president reviewed the history of persecution of the Jewish people. He believed that official proscription against the Jews remained most prevalent in Russia and Rumania. His hope was that the League of Nations would find ways that Jews could "be given equal rights and be protected in these rights, and secure the equality of opportunity through such protection."[29]

The evil effects of anti-Semitism persisted and found new expression in the turbulent years after World War I, in such scurrilous publications as the *Protocols of the Elders of Zion*, which accused the Jews of such things as horrible blood libels. The automobile manufacturer Henry Ford provided this fabricated document with extensive circulation through his newspaper, the *Dearborn Independent*.

Taft gave an address to the B'nai B'rith in Chicago on 23 December. "One of the chief causes of suffering and evil in the world today is race hatred and any man who stimulates that hatred has much to answer for," Taft informed his audience. He dismissed the charge of Jewish power over banking and industry when he noted that "more than half the 13,000,000 Jews in the world are still suffering not only persecution and oppression but the bitterest penury and starvation." And of the so-called protocols themselves, the speaker dismissed them with contempt. "The 'Tales of Baron Munchausen' are the only things in literature that should be classed with these protocols. There is not the slightest ground for antisemitism among us. It has no place in America."[30]

The next day Taft arrived in Marion, Ohio, to meet the president-elect and Mrs. Harding for a breakfast meeting that lasted until noon. They discussed White House decorum, what his friends should call Harding after the inauguration, and the makeup of the Harding cabinet. The former president offered extensive comments on the choices Harding was contemplating. As Taft reported to his wife in a letter two days later, the president-elect then said: "By the way, I want to ask you, would you accept a position on the Supreme Bench? Because if you would, I'll put you on that Court."[31]

Recalling the conversation for his wife, Taft reported that he told

Harding that a place on the Court "always had been the ambition of my life." He said that he had turned down several appointments as an associate justice in the Roosevelt administration but could no longer settle for such a place. "I was obliged to say that now under the circumstances of having been President, and having appointed three of the present bench and three others and having protested against Brandeis, I could not accept any place but the chief justiceship." Harding made no response to Taft's conditions and insistence on being the chief justice. To Nellie Taft, he said that he was "nearly struck dumb when he asked me if I would go on the Supreme Court."[32]

Perhaps Taft had been taken aback at Harding's mention of the Supreme Court, but the way in which he insisted on becoming the chief justice right at that moment suggests that he had done some thinking about possible answers should Harding raise the court question. Taft sent Harding a note of thanks on Christmas Day. In it he reiterated his stance on the possible appointment. He added as well that Chief Justice Edward D. White had often confided to Taft that "he was holding the office for me and that he would give it back to a Republican administration."[33]

Harding and Taft then talked about the racial policies of the Republicans toward African Americans. Taft advised the incoming president to "appoint no negroes south of the Mason Dixon line, because it did neither the negroes nor whites any good to make appointments of negroes where the leading element was white." Harding indicated that "he believed in a Lily White Republican Party not Black and Tan."[34] If anything, Taft's views on black Americans had regressed since his presidency.

Taft did not mention anything about the Supreme Court when he spoke with reporters after the Christmas Eve session. Instead, he emphasized that Harding, while out to "avoid the political and military obligations of the treaty and the league," remained committed to an arrangement with other nations that would promote disarmament, a world court, and an ongoing conference of nations to negotiate controversial questions that might lead to war. Taft praised the president-elect for "working out a practical solution which may not be wholly satisfactory to the enthusiasts of either extreme." Taft had further retreated a long way from his previous endorsement of the League of Nations, but of course now his judicial destiny was in the hands of the incoming president.[35]

Looking back on the episode forty-eight hours later, Taft did not "feel at all confident it will all work out as I would like it, but it is more favorable to my hope and ambition than I thought possible." Taft now began six months of waiting as Harding came into office and then launched his new administration. Gus Karger became Taft's link to the inner operations of the new White House and the president's attitude. In mid-January, he reported that Harry Daugherty had informed him of Harding's intention to select Taft for chief justice when Edward D. White stepped down or died. As Karger put it, Daugherty said "that Senator Harding had told him that he didn't care what anybody else would say about it or who Senator Knox's candidate might be, that he would appoint you Chief Justice of the United States. I had an impulse to kiss Harry when he told me so, but I fought it down."[36]

By this time White was in failing health but showed no signs of his reported intention to make way for Taft and the Republicans. Taft had to watch and wait. In late March, the *New York Times* forecast that Taft would become chief justice. Friends wrote to Taft hoping that the press report was true. He cautioned them not to get too eager and excited about his prospects. "The coincidence of so many circumstances is necessary to bring about a result like that prophesied, that I cannot permit myself to be troubled about making it possible."[37]

While he waited for his own destiny to be decided, Taft advised Harry Daugherty about judicial appointments. One aspirant would make a good judge but when Taft "saw him last, it seemed to me as if his head had been a bit swelled, and as if he was carrying on a good deal of 'side,' as the English say." Taft assured Daugherty: "You know I don't want to break in on matters of patronage, but sometimes when I can make a helpful suggestion, I venture to do so, especially in respect to the Judges, because the Federal Judiciary are like the apple of my eye."[38]

By the spring of 1921, it was evident even to Taft that Harding was not going to do much in the way of finding an alternative to the League of Nations, as he had hinted he might do in the campaign. Instead, in his inaugural address, he had stated that "a world super government is contrary to everything we cherish and can have no sanction in our Republic." In a masterpiece of understatement, Taft informed a friend that Harding "is not as favorable to the League of Nations as I am, but I am hoping that the circumstances in the world are gradually convincing him that the United States has to play a part, and that we shall drift into some such situation as that which we wish in perhaps a different form, but with substantially the same result." The vigorous proponent of the league just two years earlier had now become a tepid observer, as the president repudiated everything Taft had earlier advocated.[39]

Taft did see one long-term policy goal realized when Congress adopted a measure to provide for annual budgeting for the government. Ever since his ill-fated campaign for such a reform during his presidency, Taft had advocated a budget system to get on top of the expenses of running the country. The war had underscored the need for such a change. The outcome meant, Taft wrote, that "we are assured of a real effort to remedy a crying evil in the fiscal machinery of our government."[40]

When would Harding act to fulfill his Christmas Eve promise to the suspense-ridden Taft? To Sidney Shepard in April 1921, the eager former president pondered what might be taking the chief justice so long to step aside as he had promised to do once there was a Republican president in office. Taft mused that, when it came to actual retirement after the age of seventy, a jurist such as Chief Justice White "seems to regard it as an admission of weakness, a singing of the Nunc Dimittis, and he satisfies himself with the many reasons why the time has not come." Should White persist in hanging on, Taft was ready to accept that fate. "If the position, which I would rather have than any in the world, is not to come to me, I have no right to complain, for the Lord has been very good to me in every way, and such great good fortune as my being put in this exalted position is more than I deserve—or at least it is more than my share."[41]

Taft's good fortune in the spring of 1921 came to fruition on 19 May when White died. "In his death," Taft wrote, "the country loses one of the great men who have headed that tribunal."[42] The speculation that Taft would be named was immediate and widespread. Taft had put some conditions in his own path. He had said that no one should be named to the court who was over sixty years of age, though he had made one such appointment in the case of his old friend Horace Lurton during his presidency. Taft himself was now sixty-three and would be sixty-four during the fall of 1921.

To the dismay of Taft and his friends, the president did not make an immediate appointment of the chief justice. A Republican senator told Taft that "there is a growing feeling that Harding ought to decide matters more promptly than he does." When Gus Karger asked Harding, "Anything new in the matter of the Supreme Court," he received the terse reply: "Nothing. I am still waiting for a second vacancy." Evidently, Harding had learned that there might be a resignation of another justice and he hoped to announce two selections at one time. Then on 21 June, Harding informed Karger: "Tell the Big Chief that I am going to put that over about the first of July."[43]

While Taft waited and worried for more than a month, Harding and Harry Daugherty had pondered several other half-baked schemes that would have delayed Taft's nomination into the fall. The absurdity of such actions finally impelled the president to make the selection. On 30 June, Harding told newsmen that he had nominated Taft and that the papers conveying the selection of Taft were on the way to the Senate as the president was speaking. He credited Attorney General Daugherty with convincing him that the time to select Taft was at hand and that waiting until the fall was not wise. After Harding had finished talking, Gus Karger shook hands with him. Harding asked: "Pleased, Gus?" The correspondent responded: "Mighty happy."[44]

The White House had not told Taft of the prospect of his appointment, and he learned the news by telephone in Montreal where he was at work on the Grand Trunk valuation case. Gus Karger also sent him a telegram that read: "Your nomination went to Senate at four today." When the reporter for the *New York Times* asked him if he was pleased with what Harding had done, a laughing Taft said, "Well, you can judge that for yourself." In an official statement for the press, Taft said that "it has been the ambition of my life to be Chief Justice, but now that it is gratified I tremble to think whether I can worthily fill the position and be useful to the country."[45]

The White House hoped that the Senate would act on Taft's nomination in open session by what would have amounted to a voice vote or acclamation. That was not to be. There were no hearings as such, as had happened with Louis D. Brandeis five years earlier. Four dissenting senators insisted that the nomination be taken up in the secrecy of an executive session. The members of this small group included William E. Borah, Hiram Johnson, Robert M. La Follette, and Thomas E. Watson, a Georgia Democrat. The process took half an hour, but in that interval the protestors had their say.

Borah maintained that Taft lacked the legal qualifications to be chief justice. "You are taking a man who has spent his life in politics and putting him at the head of the greatest judicial tribunal in the world." The proponents of Taft, especially the southern Democrats, noted that as president the nominee had named Edward D. White, himself a Southerner, to the chief-justiceship. One Democrat, Ellison D. "Cotton Ed" Smith of South Carolina, said he felt obligated to vote for Taft because when he became president Taft "sent word to the people of South Carolina that the best elements of the state would be recognized in appointments for office." Smith was saying in the code words of that time that Taft had promised not to appoint African Americans to Republican patronage positions. Once everyone had their say, the Senate confirmed Taft by the vote of 61 to 4.[46]

The public reaction to Taft's selection reflected the return in esteem that he had achieved since leaving the presidency eight years earlier. It was, said one commentator in the *North American Review*, "in accord with general expectation and desire. Had the matter been submitted to a plebiscite, he would have been elected by an overwhelming majority." The *Washington Post* noted that, despite the small minority against him, "all of the great lawyers of the Senate, Republicans and Democrats, readily voted for Judge Taft." In the *American Review of Reviews*, Samuel Spring said that "deftly, tactfully, cheerfully, Mr. Taft kept himself in the public eye without creating criticism, although he had so many acrid enemies in 1912."[47]

From the liberal side of the political spectrum, the editors of the *Nation* found the choice of Taft "a mistaken appointment." They acknowledged his pleasant personal traits, but deemed selection "a grave mistake." Taft had rigid views on too many issues, had been lazy as president, and was no friend of free speech and dissenters. "It was not a Taft, but a Brandeis or a Holmes that the times called for."[48]

With the announcement of the appointment, congratulations poured in to the new chief justice. His sister conveyed "loving congratulations from Bill and me on fulfillment of mother's dream." An educator called him "the first to bring to one beloved personality the two highest public offices in the United States." One enthusiastic supporter said: "Peoples on the face of the earth to be congratulated upon your appointment as chief justice of the greatest court in the world certainly the right man in the right place."[49]

Taft reveled in the flood of congratulatory messages and favorable press comment on his nomination and confirmation. He had at last attained the place he coveted since he first started to practice law four decades earlier, and nothing was going to deprive him of the pleasure of that moment. Soon, as he said in 1925, he had put out of his memory the years when he was president, and thought only of his happiness on the bench.

The years between the presidency and the Supreme Court had been filled with the activity and travel for which Taft had become famous. He was, wrote Charles W. Duke in *Washington Herald Magazine*, "the greatest of globe trotters for humanity."[50] With the aid of Wendell Mischler, the former president had crisscrossed the country from 1913 through the summer of 1921. He might take refuge from it all during the summers at Murray Bay, but in other months of the year he was likely to be in towns large and small, speaking to every kind of audience on the law, peace, and politics.

An inveterate traveler was reinventing himself as an elder Republican statesman with no visible political ambition but to inform the public on the issues of the day. His newspaper column served much the same purpose both during the war and in the turbulent period of post-war recovery from 1919 to 1921.

In so doing, he had made his post-presidency a winning campaign to put himself back into the national political mind as an active player, rather than a repudiated chief executive. The general acclaim that greeted his appointment as chief justice emphasized the success he had achieved over the eight years of his time in private life, outside the federal government. Achieving his lifelong ambition had required some fancy political stepping, especially on the issue of the League of Nations. Had Taft behaved with more consistency and resoluteness on behalf of the league, he would not likely have changed the outcome of the treaty fight. But his handling of Warren G. Harding and the league had not shown Taft at his best as a public figure. He would have probably said it was a price he was willing to pay to advance the cause of conservatism on the Supreme Court. That he did for the next decade. Just as he soon forgot he was ever president, he also put aside the Wilson years and their compromises with his professed ideals.

Taft's eight years out of public office showed both his best and his worst qualities. As an advocate of world peace he helped to launch the League to Enforce Peace and imparted much of the energy that the organization achieved between 1915 and 1918. Taft worked at home for the war effort after 1917, and he sought industrial peace as a member of the National War Labor Board. In his service on the Lincoln Memorial Commission and as president of the American Red Cross he contributed to the success of these charitable institutions. Because of his obsession with achieving the post of chief justice of the United States in the event of a Republican presidency, Taft also indulged some of his less attractive impulses. Revenge for perceived slights during his presidency motivated his opposition to Louis D. Brandeis in 1916. His reconciliation with Theodore Roosevelt owed more to Taft's hatred for Woodrow Wilson than any real affection for his one-time friend and political partner.

In the case of the League of Nations, Taft was at war with him-self. His concern for a mechanism to implement peace after the fighting ended was sincere, and he sought for a long time to help President Wilson negotiate a treaty that could receive the approval of the United States Senate. As it became obvious that the Repub-licans would never accord Wilson a political victory by endorsing the league in 1919 and 1920, Taft fell back on partisanship in deter-mining his path. He swallowed the evasions of Warren G. Harding and did little but blame Wilson as the league slipped away. Taft's willingness to give up so much of the idea of the League of Nations raises legitimate questions about the sincerity of his belief in an international organization in the first place.

NOTES

INTRODUCTION

1. Henry F. Pringle, *The Life and Times of William Howard Taft.* 2 vols. (New York: Farrar & Rinehart, 1939).

2. Jonathan Lurie, *William Howard Taft: The Travails of a Progressive Conservative* (New York: Cambridge University Press, 2011).

3. Donald F. Anderson, *William Howard Taft: A Conservative's Conception of the Presidency* (Ithaca, N.Y.: Cornell University Press, 1968, 1973), p. viii.

4. Paolo Coletta, *The Presidency of William Howard Taft* (Lawrence: University Press of Kansas, 1973).

5. Judith Icke Anderson, *William Howard Taft: An Intimate History* (New York: W. W. Norton, 1981).

6. Lewis L. Gould, *The William Howard Taft Presidency* (Lawrence: University Press of Kansas, 2009).

7. Allen E. Ragan, *Chief Justice Taft* (Columbus: Ohio State Archaeological and Historical Society, 1938).

8. Alpheus T. Mason, *William Howard Taft: Chief Justice* (New York: Simon & Schuster, 1965).

9. David H. Burton, *Taft, Holmes and the 1920s Court: An Appraisal* (Madison, N.J.: Fairleigh Dickinson University Press, 1998), and Peter G. Renstrom, *The Taft Court: Justices, Rulings, and Legacy* (Santa Barbara, Calif.: ABC-CLIO, 2003).

CHAPTER 1. THE REJECTED PRESIDENT

1. Frederick C. Hicks, *William Howard Taft: Yale Professor of Law & New Haven Citizen* (New Haven, Conn.: Yale University Press, 1945), p. 6.

2. "Hundreds Welcome Taft at Augusta," *New York Sun*, 6 March 1913.

3. Taft to William Allen White, 28 February 1908, William Howard Taft Papers, Manuscript Division, Library of Congress (hereafter cited as WHT).

4. "Taft Back, Ruddy and Ready to Work," *New York Times*, 1 April 1913.

5. Taft to Frederick Forchheimer, 2 April 1913, WHT.

6. Lewis L. Gould, *Helen Taft: Our Musical First Lady* (Lawrence: University Press of Kansas, 2009).

7. Hicks, *William Howard Taft*, pp. 15–22.

8. Charles W. Duke, "Taft, the Greatest of Globe Trotters for Humanity," *Washington Herald*, 2 July 1921. In his article Duke quoted the photographic inscription.

9. Wendell Mischler to Taft, 7 June 1913, WHT; Taft to Charles P. Taft, 18 May 1913, WHT.

10. Gina Kolata, "In Struggle with Weight, Taft Used a Modern Diet," *New York Times*, 14 October 2013.

11. Taft to Charles P. Taft, 27 May 1913, WHT.

12. "Taft on 'Political Cranks,'" *New York Times*, 10 May 1913; "Taft Attacks the Recall," *New York Times*, 13 May 1913.

13. Taft to Howard C. Hollister, 17 May 1913, WHT; Taft to Elihu Root, 5 May 1913, WHT.

14. Taft to Mabel Boardman, 15 April 1913, Mabel Boardman Papers, Box 6, Manuscript Division, Library of Congress.

15. "Taft's Request Granted: Treasury Department Chooses Pink Marble for New Haven Court House," *New York Times*, 30 October 1913.

16. "Taft, in New Role of Lobbyist, Is Success," *Philadelphia Inquirer*, 26 September 1913. Christopher A. Thomas's *The Lincoln Memorial & American Life* (Princeton, N.J.: 2002) is an excellent survey of the political and aesthetic issues surrounding the construction of the memorial.

17. Taft to Elihu Root, 27 November 1913, WHT. For the correspondence over the marble, see Garrison to Taft, 11 October 1913, WHT; Taft to Garrison, 12 October 1913 and 15 October 1913, WHT; Taft to Woodrow Wilson, 19 November 1913, WHT; Garrison to Taft, 10 January 1914 and 14 January 1914, WHT.

18. Democratic National Committee, *The Democratic Text-Book, 1912* (New York: 1912), p. 30.

19. William Howard Taft, "Our Duty to the Philippines," *Independent* 76 (16 October 1913): p. 118.

20. On the snubbing incident, see "Taft Bars Harrison from His Presence," *New York Times*, 10 June 1910. Harrison had remarried after his first wife's death, to a woman who was newly divorced in what Washington society regarded as unseemly haste. "Harrison Named for Philippines," *New York Times*, 21 August 1913. Taft to William Cameron Forbes, 3 October 1913, WHT. Harrison discussed the circumstances of his appointment in his *The Corner-Stone of Philippine Independence: A Narrative of Seven Years* (New York: The Century Co., 1922), pp. 3–6. Peter W. Stanley, *A Nation in the Making: The Philippines and the United States, 1899–1921* (Cambridge, Mass.: Harvard University Press, 1974), pp. 201–207, gives useful historical background on the Harrison administration.

21. "Too Soon to Free Filipino, Says Taft," *New-York Tribune*, 11 June 1913.

22. Taft to Martin Egan, 3 October 1913 (first quotation), WHT; Taft to Richard E. Forrest, 12 October 1913 (third quotation), WHT; Harrison, *The Corner-Stone of Philippine Independence*, p. 50 (second quotation); "Hold the Islands Is Taft's Plea," *New-York Tribune*, 20 November 1913.

23. "Carabao Report to Wilson," *New York Times*, 19 December 1913.

24. "Defends the Carabao: Taft Says Its Songs Do Not Reflect Army's Attitude," *Washington Post*, 20 December 1913; "Taft Makes Light of Carabao Gibes," *New York Times*, 20 December 1913.

25. Woodrow Wilson to Henry Jones Ford, 23 January 1914, in Arthur S.

Link et al., eds., *The Papers of Woodrow Wilson: Volume 29* (Princeton, N.J.: Princeton University Press, 1979), p. 164.

26. "Taft Delivers Main Address at Montreal," *Duluth News-Tribune*, 3 September 1913; Taft to Will Herron, 26 August 1913, WHT.

27. Roscoe Pound to Taft, 13 June 1913, WHT; Henry M. Bates to Taft, 10 June 1913, WHT. For Pound's campaign to change the way law was taught and lawyers trained, see William M. Wiecek, *The Lost World of Classical Legal Thought: Law and Ideology in America, 1886–1937* (New York: Oxford University Press, 1998), pp. 191–192.

28. Taft to Will Herron, 24 August 1913, WHT.

29. Taft to Charles P. Taft, 11 September 1913, WHT.

30. Ibid.

31. Jacob M. Dickinson, "To the members of the American Bar Association," April 12, 1913, pamphlet in author's collection. Jerold S. Auerbach, *Unequal Justice: Lawyers and Social Change in Modern America* (New York: Oxford University Press, 1976), pp. 65–66.

32. Henry St. George Tucker to Taft, 22 November 1913, WHT.

33. *American Bar Association: Speeches at Banquet, Montreal Canada, September 3, 1913* (n.p., n.d., but 1913), copy in author's collection; Taft to Charles P. Taft, 11 September 1913, WHT. Richard Burdon Haldane, "Higher Nationality," U.S. Senate, Document No. 233, 63 Cong., 1 Sess. (Washington: 1913).

34. Taft to George Whitelock, 29 September 1913, WHT.

35. Taft to James DeWitt Andrews, 8 November 1913, WHT.

36. Taft to Richard Haldane, 13 November 1913, WHT.

37. E. R. Thayer to Taft, 13 November 1913, WHT.

38. Max Pam to Taft, 2 December 1913, WHT.

39. J. H. Choate to Taft, 19 November 1913; Haldane to Taft, 26 November 1913, WHT.

40. Taft to Edward Douglass White, 7 January 1914, WHT; Taft to Albert Bettinger, 7 January 1914, WHT.

41. Taft to Mabel Boardman, 26 February 1913, Box 6, Boardman Papers.

42. Elizabeth Brown Pryor, *Clara Barton: Professional Angel* (Philadelphia: University of Pennsylvania Press, 1987), pp. 332–333, looks at the origins of Boardman's opposition to Barton's control of the Red Cross. Marian Moser Jones, *The American Red Cross from Clara Barton to the New Deal* (Baltimore, Md.: Johns Hopkins University Press, 2013), is a thorough new account of the Red Cross that does justice to the Barton-Boardman controversy. Julia F. Irwin, *Making the World Safe: The American Red Cross and a Nation's Humanitarian Awakening* (New York: Oxford University Press, 2013), pp. 28–30, also considers the Boardman-Barton dispute.

43. Mabel T. Boardman, "Red Cross's Urgent Need for New Quarters," *New York Times*, 9 November 1913.

44. Taft to Boardman, 12 October 1913, WHT; "The Red Cross Memorial," *New York Times*, 31 October 1913.

45. Taft to Mrs. Russell Sage, 29 October 1913, WHT; J. J. Slocum to Taft, 26 November 1913 (discussing the donation on behalf of Mrs. Sage), WHT; "Red Cross to Get a $700,000 Home," *New-York Tribune*, 11 December 1913.

46. Helen Woodrow Bones to Jessie Woodrow Bones Brewer, 7 June 1913, in Arthur S. Link et al., eds., *The Papers of Woodrow Wilson* (Princeton, N.J.: Princeton University Press), pp. 561–562.

47. Karger to Taft, 2 August 1913, WHT.

48. Taft to Elihu Root, 5 May 1913, WHT.

49. Taft to Charles Sidney Shepard, 6 July 1913, WHT.

50. Taft to Charles D. Hilles, 28 July 1913, sending some draft language for the article.

51. Taft to Robert A. Taft, 20 November 1913, WHT.

52. Taft to Charles D. Hilles, 7 September 1913, WHT; Taft to Gus Karger, 17 September 1913, WHT; Taft to Horace Taft, 26 October 1913, WHT.

53. Helen Taft, *Recollections of Full Years* (New York: Dodd, Mead, 1914).

54. Taft to Walter L. Fisher, 3 January 1914, WHT.

CHAPTER 2. "WAR IS A DREADFUL THING"

1. "Law and Laughs Mixed by Taft," *Washington Herald*, 4 January 1914.

2. There is a good discussion of Taft's teaching methods in Frederick C. Hicks, *William Howard Taft: Yale Professor of Law & New Haven Citizen* (New Haven: Yale University Press, 1945), pp. 39–45.

3. "Law and Laughs Mixed By Taft."

4. Taft to Mabel Boardman, 10 February 1914, WHT.

5. Taft to Robert A. Taft, 16 January 1914, WHT.

6. William Howard Taft, "The College Slouch. Where Did It Come From? What Does It Indicate? Where May It Lead a Boy?" *Ladies' Home Journal*, May 1914, p. 13. See also *Cornell Daily Sun*, 13 May 1914.

7. Taft to H. L. Merry, 14 February 1914; Taft to Charles P. Taft, 14 February 1914; Taft to Louis E. Stoddard, 14 February 1914, WHT.

8. Taft to Charles P. Taft, 18 February 1914, WHT.

9. Charles W. Duke, "Taft, The Greatest of Globe Trotters for Humanity: New Chief Justice Noted as the Most Traveled Man in Public Life," *Washington Herald Magazine of Features and Fiction*, 2 July 1921. *Taft and Roosevelt: The Intimate Letters of Archie Butt, Military Aide.* 2 vols. (Garden City, N.Y.: Doubleday, Doran, 1930), vol. 1, p. 316.

10. "Taft Warns Canada," *The New York Times*, 1 February 1914; Taft to Mabel Boardman, 10 February 1914, WHT.

11. Taft to Boardman, 10 February 1914, WHT.

12. William Howard Taft, "The Future of the Republican Party," *Saturday Evening Post*, February 14, 1914.

13. "Taft-Roosevelt Feud Still Bitter," *Washington Times*, 11 February 1914; "Taft Says Mr. Wilson Will Be Re-Elected," *Washington Herald*, 13 February 1914. "Mr. Taft's Point of View," *Washington Herald*, 15 February 1914, stated that Taft's position would ensure Woodrow Wilson's re-election.

14. Taft to Martin Egan, 18 February 1914, WHT; "Taft Out of Office Fight," *Washington Herald*, 13 February 1914.

15. Taft to Gus Karger, 3 March 1914, WHT. "Ready to Build Memorial," *New York Times*, 9 February 1914.

16. "From Former President of the United States, Wm. H. Taft," *New York Times*, 8 June 1913; "From William H. Taft," *Life*, 2 October 1913. A good recent review of Taft's position on arbitration during his presidency is by John E. Noyes, "William Howard Taft and the Taft Arbitration Treaties," *Villanova Law Review* 56 (2011): 535–558.

17. William H. Short to Taft, 23 September 1913 (two letters), WHT. Warren F. Kuehl, *Seeking World Order: The United States and International Or-*

ganization to 1920 (Nashville, Tenn.: Vanderbilt University Press, 1969), pp. 181–182.

18. William Howard Taft, "Shall the Federal Government Protect Aliens in Their Treaty Rights?" *Independent* 77 (February 2, 1914): pp. 156–158.

19. William Howard Taft, "Why Not Arbitrate Everything," *Independent* 77 (16 March 1914): pp. 379–381.

20. Ibid., p. 381.

21. William Howard Taft, "Experiments in Federation for Judicial Settlements of International Disputes," *Independent* 78 (13 April 1914): pp. 88–90; William Howard Taft, "The Promise of World Federation," *Independent* 78 (20 April 1914): pp. 136–138.

22. C. R. Maccauley, "A Business Day with Mr. Taft in New Haven," *New York Sun,* 22 March 1914.

23. Taft to Mrs. Eugene Stafford, 9 July 1914, WHT.

24. Taft to Helen Herron Taft, 7 June 1914, WHT. Taft to J. A. Hemenway, 14 June 1914, J. A. Hemenway Papers, Manuscripts Division, Lilly Library, Indiana University–Bloomington.

25. Charles Warren Fairbanks, "President Taft's Visit—June 6, 1914," Charles Warren Fairbanks Papers, Manuscripts Department, Lilly Library, Indiana University–Bloomington, pp. 6, 9.

26. William Howard Taft," A Message to the People of the United States," *Independent* 79 (10 August 1914): pp. 198–199. Henry F. Pringle, *The Life and Times of William Howard Taft,* 2 vols. (New York, 1939), vol. 2, pp. 871–872, cites this message as a letter to the journal's editor, Hamilton Holt, and concludes that his subject was "publicly silent" about the war in these early days and weeks.

27. Elihu Root to Taft, 12 September 1914, WHT.

28. Taft to editor of the *New York American,* 12 September 1914, James Creelman to Taft, 12 September 1914, Taft to Creelman, 14, September 1914, WHT.

29. May Childs Nerney to Taft, 14 September 1914; Hollis B. Fissell to Taft, 3 October 1914, WHT.

30. Taft to James C. Waters, Jr., 12 July 1915, WHT.

31. Taft to Simon P. W. Drew, 28 November 1915, WHT.

32. Remarks of William H. Taft at the National Press Club, 19 October 1914, WHT.

33. Ibid. For coverage of the event, see "Taft Glad He's on the Outside," *Washington Herald,* 19 October 1914 (last quotation); "Taft Happier Now Than as President," *New York Sun,* 19 October 1914.

34. "Taft Urges Law to Guard Aliens," *New York Times,* 21 October 1914. William Howard Taft, "Recent Antitrust and Labor Injunction Legislation: Annual Address Delivered before the American Bar Association at the Annual Meeting Held on October 20, 1914, at Washington, D.C." For the full text of Taft's speech, see Senate Document 614, 63 Cong., 2d Sess. (Washington, D. C.: Government Printing Office, 1914), pp. 3–4.

35. Taft, "Recent Antitrust and Labor Injunction Legislation," pp. 17–18.

36. Karger to Taft, 17 September 1914, WHT.

37. Theodore Roosevelt to Meyer Lissner, 16 November 1914, Theodore Roosevelt Papers, Manuscript Division, Library of Congress.

38. Taft to Myron Herrick, 14 December 1914, WHT.

39. "Taft Opposes Plea for Big Armament," *New York Times,* 5 December 1914; "Taft Would Keep Our Force Efficient," *New York Times,* 10 December 1914; "Taft Opposes Ban on Arms," *New York Times,* 10 February 1915.

40. These two paragraphs are based on the discussion in Ruhl J. Barlett, *The League to Enforce Peace* (Chapel Hill, N.C.: University of North Carolina Press, 1944), pp. 36–37.

41. "United States Must Act at Once on Lusitania, Says Colonel Roosevelt," *New York Times*, 10 May 1915; "Wickersham Would Discipline Germany," *New York Times*, 10 May 1915.

42. Taft to Clarence H. Kelsey, 15 May 1915, WHT.

43. "Taft at White House," *New York Times*, 20 October 1914.

44. Taft to Wilson, 10 May 1915, WHT.

45. Wilson to Taft, 13 May 1915, in Arthur S. Link et al., eds., *The Papers of Woodrow Wilson*, vol. 33, *April 17–July 21, 1915* (Princeton, N. J.: Princeton University Press, 1980), p. 184.

46. "Address before the Union League of Philadelphia," 11 May 1915; Taft to Karger, 15 May 1915, WHT.

47. "Taft Heads Move for Peace League," *New York Times*, 31 May 1915.

48. Ibid.; "Remarks at a Press Conference," 8 June 1915, *Papers of Woodrow Wilson, Volume 33*, pp. 368–369.

49. "League to Enforce Peace Is Launched," *New York Times*, 18 June 1915; William Howard Taft, "A Restraint upon War," *Independent* 82 (14 June 1915): 459–460. See also: League to Enforce Peace, American Branch, *Independence Hall Conference Held in the City of Philadelphia Bunker Hill Day (June 17th), 1915, Together with the Speeches Made at a Public Banquet in the Bellevue-Stratford Hotel on the Preceding Evening* (New York, N.Y.: League to Enforce Peace, 1915).

50. Taft to Karger, 14 April 1915, WHT.

51. Taft to Mrs. Buckner Wallingford, 25 May 1915, WHT. Ironically, Roosevelt also believed that the rulings of the trial judge had prevented him from putting on his strongest case against Barnes. Roosevelt to Archibald Bulloch Roosevelt, 19 May 1915, Theodore Roosevelt Papers, Manuscript Division, Library of Congress.

52. Taft to Delia Torrey, 12 June 1915, WHT.

CHAPTER 3. STRAINS ON THE TAFT-WHITE RELATIONSHIP, 1915–1916

1. William Howard Taft to Horace Taft, 22 June 1915, William Howard Taft Papers, Manuscript Division, Library of Congress (hereafter cited as WHT).

2. Taft to Horace Taft, 2 July 1913, WHT. Philippe Dube, *Charlevoix: Two Centuries at Murray Bay* (Kingston & Montreal, 1989), pp. 99–101, is the best brief account for Taft's life at Murray Bay and is the source of the family poem.

3. Taft to Gus Karger, 3 July 1915, WHT; Taft to Mabel Boardman, 16 July 1915, and 24 July 1915, WHT.

4. Taft to Jacob M. Dickinson, 6 July 1915, WHT; "Orders Rock Island Directors Sued," *New York Times*, 15 September 1915.

5. William Howard Taft, "The Military and Naval Defenses of the United States: What They Are—What They Should Be," *Saturday Evening Post* 187 (5 June 1915): p. 38.

6. Mabel Boardman to Taft, 27 September 1914, WHT. *Eleventh Annual Report of the American National Red Cross for the Year 1915*, U.S. Congress, House of Representatives, 64 Cong., 1 Sess., Document 1307 (Washington, D.C.: Government Printing Office, 1916), pp. 5, 9.

7. "Red Cross Units to be Recalled," *New York Times*, 26 July 1915.

8. Taft to Boardman, 1 November 1915, WHT.

9. *Eleventh Annual Report*, p. 5; Jones, *The American Red Cross*, pp. 162–163; Taft to Mabel Boardman, 1 November 1915, WHT.

10. Taft to Mabel Boardman, 29 July 1915, WHT.

11. *Government of the Philippines*, U.S. Senate Committee on the Philippines, 63 Cong., 3 Sess. (2 January 1915), p. 366; "Filipinos Unfit to Rule Isles, Taft Declares," *Washington Herald*, 3 January 1915; "Taft Puts 60 Year Limit on Filipino Rule," *New York Sun*, 3 January 1915.

12. "Remarks at a Press Conference," 30 March 1915, in Arthur S. Link et al., eds., *The Papers of Woodrow Wilson*, vol. 33 (Princeton, N.J.: Princeton University Press, 1979), pp. 456–457.

13. Francis Burton Harrison to Joseph P. Tumulty, 31 August 1915, in Arthur S. Link et al., eds., *The Papers of Woodrow Wilson*, vol. 34, *July 21–September 30, 1915* (Princeton, N.J.: Princeton University Press, 1980), pp. 390–391.

14. "Taft Denounces Our Filipino Policy," *New York Times*, 7 September 1915.

15. Ibid.

16. "Answer to Taft Is 'Filipinization,'" *Washington Times*, 7 September 1915.

17. "Says Filipinos Are Governed in Worst Way," *New York Sun*, 9 November 1915; "Taft Sees Wreck of Philippine Rule," *New York Times*, 11 November 1915.

18. "Links Taft in Deceit: Ex-President Endorsed Mendacity on Philippines, Says Garrison," *Washington Post*, 30 November 1915; "Says Taft Is Partisan: Ex-President's Philippine Witness Discredited by Secretary Garrison," *New York Times*, 30 November 1915.

19. "Taft Clashes with Garrison over Filipinos," *New York Tribune*, 30 November 1915.

20. O. Garfield Jones, *The Unhappy Conditions in the Philippines: An account of the disorganization of the government and a description of the misrule of the Filipino people through the policy of "spoils for the deserving" enforced by President Woodrow Wilson and Governor-General Francis Burton Harrison* (Oakland, Calif.: Oakland Tribune, 1915); "Unjust, Says Taft: Ex-President, Denying Partisanship, Resents Secretary Garrison's Attack," *New York Times*, 30 November 1915.

21. "No Party Question," *New York Sun*, 1 December 1915; "Garrison Again Assails Taft," *New York Times*, 2 December 1915; "Garrison Guilty as Issue Dodger, Taft Declares," *New York Tribune*, 7 December 1915.

22. Karger to Taft, 1 December 1915, WHT.

23. William Howard Taft, "The Democratic Record," *Yale Review* 6 (October 1916): 12–13.

24. Taft to Helen Taft, 12 April 1918, WHT. "A Philippine Survey," 11 February 1921, in James F. Vivian, ed., *William Howard Taft: Collected Editorials, 1917–1921* (New York, N.Y.: Praeger, 1990), p. 539.

25. Taft to John C. Robertson, 14 January 1914, WHT; Taft to Jacob M. Dickinson, 18 January 1914, WHT.

26. Thomas B. Love to Albert S. Burleson, 3 February 1916, Thomas B. Love Papers, Dallas Historical Society; "Taft Refuses to Comment," *Washington Post*, 29 January 1916. Melvin I. Urofsky, *Louis D. Brandeis: A Life* (New York: Pantheon Books, 2009), p. 438, says that Taft "thought for some reason that Wilson would appoint him." I have found no evidence that Taft ever believed

it was conceivable that Wilson, a Democrat, might select his Republican predecessor for the Supreme Court. Taft was flattered when people suggested his name, and would have given the nomination serious consideration had Wilson named him. However, he knew it would not occur.

27. Lewis L. Gould, *The William Howard Taft Presidency* (Lawrence: University Press of Kansas, 2009), pp. 70–71, 76, 77.

28. Taft to George Whitlock, 29 September 1913, WHT.

29. *Taft and Roosevelt: The Intimate Letters of Archie Butt.* 2 vols. (Garden City, N.Y.: Doubleday, Doran, 1930), vol. 1, p. 38.

30. Taft to Herman Bernstein, 27 March 1916, WHT. See also William Howard Taft, "The Progressive World Struggle of the Jews for Civil Equality," *National Geographic Magazine* 36 (July 1919): 1–23.

31. Taft to Charles P. Taft, 12 October 1916, WHT.

32. Taft to Karger, 31 January 1916, WHT.

33. Taft to Henry Waters Taft, 31 January 1916. Urofsky, *Louis D. Brandeis*, pp. 399–430, considers how Brandeis gained a leadership role among American Zionists.

34. Taft to Henry Waters Taft, 31 January 1916.

35. Karger to Taft, 22 February 1916, WHT.

36. Karger to Taft, 8 March 1916, WHT.

37. "Taft Opposes Brandeis," *New York Times*, 15 March 1916; Taft to Louis A. Coolidge, 14 March 1916, WHT.

38. "Powerful Brandeis Protest," *Washington Times*, 16 March 1916.

39. For Lippmann, see Todd, *Justice on Trial*, p. 179; "Truth: Coming Out of Mr. Taft and Mr. Root against Mr. Brandeis," *Harper's Weekly*, 1 April 1916, p. 324; "Taft vs. Brandeis," *Harper's Weekly*, 8 April 1916, pp. 359–360; Florence Kelley, "Mr. Brandeis," *Survey* 36 (13 May 1916): p. 191.

40. Taft to George Wickersham, 27 March 1916, WHT. Todd, *Justice on Trial*, pp. 179–180.

41. Arthur Dehon Hill to Henry Cabot Lodge, 31 January 1916, Henry Cabot Lodge Papers, Massachusetts Historical Society, Boston.

42. Taft to Wilson, 11 April 1916, in Arthur S. Link et al., eds., *The Papers of Woodrow Wilson*, vol. 35, *January 27–May 8, 1916* (Princeton, N.J.: Princeton University Press, 1981), p. 459.

43. Ibid., Taft to Wilson, 11 April 1916, p. 459; Wilson to Taft, 14 April 1916, p. 481.

44. Ibid., p. 545.

45. Wilson to Taft, 18 May 1916, WHT. For the reasons animating Wilson's change of heart, see Justus Doencke, *Nothing Less Than War: A New History of America's Entry into World War I* (Lexington: University Press of Kentucky, 2011), pp. 179–181.

46. "Taft Creates Mild Furore at White House Tea Party," *Washington Herald*, 27 May 1916. The *Washington Star*, 27 May 1916, quoted in League to Enforce Peace, *Enforced Peace: Proceedings of the First Annual National Assemblage of the League to Enforce Peace, Washington, May 26–27, 1916* (New York: League to Enforce Peace, 1916), p. 3.

47. "An Address to the League to Enforce Peace, May 27, 1916," in Arthur S. Link et al., eds., *The Papers of Woodrow Wilson*, vol. 37, *May 9–August 7, 1916* (Princeton, N.J.: Princeton University Press, 1981), p. 116.

48. Taft to J. H. Patterson, 28 May 1916, WHT.

49. Thomas J. Knock, *To End All Wars: Woodrow Wilson and the Quest for a New World Order* (Princeton, N.J.: Princeton University Press, 1992), p. 78.

CHAPTER 4. THE ELECTION OF 1916 AND AMERICAN ENTRY INTO THE WAR

1. Taft to Louis A. Coolidge, 20 March 1916, William Howard Taft Papers, Manuscript Division, Library of Congress (hereafter cited as WHT).

2. See Roosevelt's statement of 9 March 1916 in Elting E. Morison et al., eds., *Letters of Theodore Roosevelt*, 8 vols. (Cambridge, Mass.: Harvard University Press, 1951–1954), p. 1024, note 1.

3. Taft to Mr. Rohrabach, 31 January 1916, WHT; Taft to David Baird, 6 March 1916, WHT.

4. Taft to Charles Evans Hughes, 8 January 1914, WHT. The Minnesota case was indeed one that demonstrated the skill of Hughes as a framer of the Court's opinions. See Alexander M. Bickel and Benno C. Schmidt, Jr., *The Oliver Wendell Holmes Devise History of the Supreme Court of the United States*, vol. 9, *The Judiciary and Responsible Government, 1910–1921* (New York: Macmillan, 1984), pp. 254–264.

5. Taft to David Baird, 6 March 1916, WHT.

6. A. L. Todd, *Justice on Trial: The Case of Louis D. Brandeis* (New York: McGraw-Hill, 1961), p. 196.

7. "Taft Will Stump Land for Hughes," *New York Tribune*, 1 July 1916.

8. "Roosevelt Dines with Hughes; Taft and T.R. to Stump," *New York Times*, 29 June 1916.

9. "Taft and Hughes in Talk about T.R.," *New York Times*, 1 July 1916.

10. "Roosevelt Sticks to Five Speeches," *New York Times*, 13 September 1916.

11. "Taft and T.R. Bury Hatchet Oct. 3," *New York Sun*, 22 September 1916; "Colonel and Taft Will End Old Feud," *New York Times*, 22 September 1916; "Roosevelt-Taft Feud Ends Oct. 3," *New York Tribune*, 22 September 1916.

12. "Roosevelt to Give Cold Hand to Taft," *New York Times*, 30 September 1916.

13. "The Shake Funeral," *New York Times*, 2 October 1916; "'Theodore' Grasps the Hand of 'Will,'" *New York Times*, 4 October 1916.

14. "Taft and Roosevelt Meeting Exceeds All Hopes of Promoters," *Washington Times*, 4 October 1916; "Finds Taft Did Not Slap Colonel's Back," *New York Times*, 5 October 1916; Clarence H. Kelsey to Taft, 4 October 1916, WHT.

15. John C. O'Laughlin to Theodore Roosevelt, 29 August 1916, Theodore Roosevelt Papers, Manuscript Division, Library of Congress.

16. Karger to Taft, 14 September 1916, WHT; Taft to Mabel Boardman, 23 October 1916, WHT. Robert A. Taft to Taft, 16 October 1916, in Clarence Wunderlin et al., eds., *The Papers of Robert A. Taft*, vol. 1, *1889–1939* (Kent, Ohio: Kent State University Press, 1997), p. 104.

17. Taft to Charles P. Taft, 12 October 1916, WHT.

18. "Taft Hits Wilson's 8-Hour Law Efforts," *New York Times*, 5 October 1916.

19. William Howard Taft, "The Democratic Record," *Yale Review* 6 (October 1916): p. 3.

20. Ibid., p. 19.

21. Ibid., p. 25.

22. Taft to Charles P. Taft, 12 October 1916, WHT; Karger to Taft, 16 October 1916, WHT; Taft to Mabel Boardman, 23 October 1916, WHT.

23. "Crowd Hoots Taft and He Stops Speech," *New York Times*, 7 November 1916.

24. Taft to Mabel Boardman, 14 November 1916, WHT; Arthur Willert to Geoffrey Robinson [Dawson], 14 October 1916, Archives of *The Times* (London).

25. Taft to Boardman, 14 November 1916, WHT.

26. Ibid.

27. "Taft Points U.S. Duty," *Washington Post*, 20 January 1917.

28. "Taft Calls Wilson's Peace Appeal an Epoch in Foreign Policy of U.S.," *Washington Post*, 26 January 1917; Thomas J. Knock, *To End All Wars: Woodrow Wilson and the Quest for a New World Order* (Princeton, N.J., Princeton University Press, 1992), p. 112.

29. Taft to Winthrop Murray Crane, 23 January 1917, WHT.

30. Roosevelt to Henry Sturgis Drinker, 9 January 1917, Theodore Roosevelt Papers, Manuscript Division, Library of Congress; Theodore Roosevelt, "The League to Enforce Peace," *Metropolitan Magazine*, February 1917, pp. 15–16, 66–67; "Taft Calls Colonel Hazy on Peace Plan," *New York Times*, 21 January 1917.

31. William C. Widenor, *Henry Cabot Lodge and the Search for an American Foreign Policy* (Berkeley: University of California Press, 1980), p. 258. For an example of the Republican suspicion of the League to Enforce Peace and Taft's sponsorship of the idea, see the discussion about the organization in the Senate on 29 January. U.S. Senate, *Congressional Record*, 64th Cong., 2d Sess. (29 January 1917): pp. 2155–2157.

32. "Mr. Taft Advocates a Conscription Law," *New York Times*, 5 February 1917; "Taft for New Policy," *Washington Post*, 7 February 1917; "Taft Would Give Son to Stop World War," *New York Times*, 24 February 1917.

33. "Taft to Make Tour," *Washington Times*, 16 March 1917.

34. Taft to Newton D. Baker, 6 February 1917, and Baker to Taft, in Arthur S. Link et al., eds., *The Papers of Woodrow Wilson*, vol. 41 (Princeton, N.J.: Princeton University Press, 1934), pp. 154–156.

35. Taft to James Bryce, 9 April 1917, WHT.

36. "Miss Taft a College Dean," *New York Times*, 24 May 1917; Taft to Delia Torrey, 31 May 1917, WHT; Taft to Katherine Wulsin, 26 November 1917, WHT.

37. Taft to Charles P. Taft, 30 May 1917, WHT; Taft to Katherine Wulsin, 26 November 1917, WHT.

38. Taft to Horace Taft, 19 September 1916, WHT.

39. Taft to Mabel Boardman, 23 October 1916, WHT.

40. Taft to Boardman, 9 April 1917, WHT; Taft to Elihu Root, 9 April 1917, WHT.

41. "Taft at the White House," *New York Times*, 29 April 1917; Woodrow Wilson to Taft, 10 May 1917, Woodrow Wilson Papers, Manuscript Division, Library of Congress.

42. Walter Prescott Webb and Terrell Webb, eds., *Washington Wife: Journal of Ellen Maury Slayden, 1897–1919* (New York: Harper & Row, 1962), p. 303.

43. "War Brunt Is Ours Now, Says Pershing," *New York Times*, 26 May 1917 (first two quotations); "U.S. Fights Teuton People, Says Taft," *Washington Post*, 20 December 1917.

44. Taft to the Secretary of the YMCA, New London, Connecticut, 10 July 1917; Taft to Gus Karger, 30 July 1917, WHT.

45. Taft to Henry L. Higginson, 2 July 1917, WHT.

46. Taft to J. W. Delamar, 12 July 1917, WHT.

47. Taft to Jacob G. Schmidlapp, 25 July 1917, WHT.

48. Taft to Woodrow Wilson, 8 August 1917, Case File 156, Wilson Papers; "Taft Gains after Unfavorable Day," *Washington Post*, 10 August 1917 (second quotation); Taft Is Cheerful and Much Better," *Washington Post*, 11 August 1917; "Taft Praises Wilson Note," *Washington Post*, 30 August 1917, giving statement sent from Canada.

49. "Taft Puts Quietus to a Pacifist Move," *New York Times*, 27 September 1917.

50. Ibid.; "Taft Aids Defeat of Pacifists at Church Congress," *Washington Times*, 27 September 1917.

51. "Taft Puts Quietus to a Pacifist Move," *New York Times*; "The Taft-Holmes Debate," The Tapestry of Faith Lifespan Curriculum, www.uua.org /re/tapestry/adults/resistance/workshop5/workshopplan/stories/182323; Steve Edington, "The President and the Pacifist," October 26, 2008, www.uu nashua.org/sermons/president and pacifist.shtml, offer Unitarian interpretations of these events.

52. James F. Vivian, ed., *William Howard Taft, Collected Editorials, 1917–1921* (New York: Praeger, 1990), pp. xv–xvii, is the source for this paragraph. Vivian's edition of Taft's columns is a major contribution to the literature on its subject's activities between the presidency and the Supreme Court.

CHAPTER 5. FROM FOURTEEN POINTS TO THE 1918 ELECTION

1. James F. Vivian, ed., *William Howard Taft: Collected Editorials, 1917–1921* (New York: Praeger, 1990), p. 3; "German Mind Must Change, Says Taft," *New York Times*, 10 January 1918; "Taft Asks Firing Squad," *Washington Post*, 22 February 1918.

2. "Fight for Lasting Peace: Taft Replies to Questions Put to Him by the Y. M. C. A.," *New York Times*, 30 June 1917; "It Is the Side That Has the Nerve That Will Win This War, Says Taft," *Macon Telegraph*, 1 March 1918, describing a thirty-day tour that Taft made of "cantonments" during the winter of 1918. See also "Camp Lee Men Salute Taft," *Washington Post*, 27 January 1918 and "Futile to End War Now, Asserts Taft," *Washington Post*, 2 February 1918. C. Howard Hopkins, *John R. Mott, 1865–1955: A Biography* (Grand Rapids, Mich.: William B. Eerdmans, 1979) is disappointing on Taft's wartime work for the YMCA.

3. "Taft Likes Draft Army," *New York Times*, 16 February 1918; Taft to Helen Taft, 7 February 1918, William Howard Taft Papers, Manuscript Division, Library of Congress (hereafter cited as WHT).

4. Taft to Katherine Wulsin, 22 April 1918, in Gary Ness, ed., "William Howard Taft and the Great War," *Cincinnati Historical Society Bulletin* 34 (1976): p. 10.

5. "A Memorandum of an Interview with William Howard Taft, 12 December 1917," in Arthur S. Link et al., eds., *The Papers of Woodrow Wilson*, vol. 45, *November 11, 1917–January 15, 1918* (Princeton, N. J.: Princeton University Press, 1984), p. 272.

6. Ibid.

7. Ruhl J. Bartlett, *The League to Enforce Peace* (Chapel Hill: University of North Carolina Press, 1944), p. 92.

8. Wilson to Edward M. House, 20 March 1918, in Arthur S. Link et al., eds., *The Papers of Woodrow Wilson*, vol. 47, *1918* (Princeton, N.J.: Princeton University Press, 1984), p. 85, has the butters-in remark; "A Memorandum by William Howard Taft," Link et al., vol. 45, p. 199.

9. Ibid., pp. 201–202.

10. Taft to Thomas Walter Bickett, 30 October 1918, WHT; William Howard Taft to William Gorham Rice, 12 April 1918, WHT.

11. "League for Victory to Bring Peace," *New York Times*, 17 May 1918.

12. Wilson to Abbott Lawrence Lowell, 11 July 1918, in Arthur S. Link et al., eds., *The Papers of Woodrow Wilson*, vol. 48, *May 13–July 17, 1918* (Princeton, N.J.: Princeton University Press, 1985), pp. 590–591.

13. Taft to William G. McAdoo, 23 September 1918, WHT.

14. Winthrop Murray Crane to Taft, 11 July 1918, Winthrop Murray Crane Papers, Massachusetts Historical Society, Boston.

15. Joseph A. McCartin, *Labor's Great War: The Struggle for Industrial Democracy and the Origins of Modern Labor Relations, 1912–1921* (Chapel Hill, N.C.: University of North Carolina Press, 1997), pp. 39–63, is excellent on the background of labor relations during World War I.

16. Maria Eucharia Meehan, "Frank P. Walsh and the American Labor Movement," (PhD diss., New York University, 1962), p. 75.

17. Taft to Charles P. Taft, 4 August 1918, WHT.

18. Taft to Katherine Wulsin, 30 May 1918, 4 July 1918, in Ness, "Taft and the Great War," pp. 13, 18. Lares and Penates were Roman household gods that protected a family's residence. In essence, Taft was saying that he was moving his effects to Washington, D.C.

19. Taft to Helen Taft, 29 March 1918, WHT.

20. The panel's recommendations are set out in Henry F. Pringle, *The Life and Times of William Howard Taft*, 2 vols. (New York: Farrar & Rinehart, 1939), vol. 2, p. 918.

21. Ibid., p. 918.

22. Wilson to Taft, 2 April 1918, WHT; Taft to Woodrow Wilson, 9 April 1918, Series 4, Case File 156, Papers of Woodrow Wilson, Manuscript Division, Library of Congress. "Wilson Creates U.S. War Labor Board," *Washington Post*, 10 April 1918. In addition to the works previously cited, Valerie Jean Conner, *The National War Labor Board: Stability, Social Justice and the Voluntary State in World War I* (Chapel Hill: University of North Carolina Press, 1983), provides an excellent overall account of the board that explains Taft's crucial role in rich detail.

23. Pringle, *Taft*, vol. 2, p. 922.

24. Basil Manly to Taft, 21 August 1919, WHT. For a similar expression of congratulation for Taft's fairness by an NWLB staffer, see Adam Wilkinson to Taft, 2 August 1919, WHT.

25. Connor, *The National War Labor Board*, pp. 35–49, provides a good brief summary of the Western Union episode.

26. Gilson Gardner, "Laboring People Now for Ex-President Taft," *Dallas Dispatch*, 6 September 1918, clipping in WHT.

27. Taft to Katherine Wulsin, 16 July 1918, in Ness, "Taft and the Great War," p. 19.

28. Will H. Hays, "The Republican Position," *Forum* 60 (August 1918): p. 136. Will Hays to Winthrop Murray Crane, 20 February 1918, Winthrop Murray Crane Papers, Massachusetts Historical Society, Boston.

29. Taft to Theodore Roosevelt, 4 February 1918, Theodore Roosevelt Papers, Manuscript Division, Library of Congress (hereafter cited as Roosevelt Papers).

30. Roosevelt to Taft, 4 March 1918 (quotation), 6 March 1918, Roosevelt Papers.

31. Roosevelt to Taft, 5 June 1918, Roosevelt Papers.

32. "Roosevelt Grips the Hand of Taft," *New York Times*, 27 May 1918. The reconciliation had been forecast the day before. "Colonel and Taft Bury the Hatchet," *New York Times*, 26 May 1918.

33. "'Delighted' Says T. R. at Meeting Taft," *New York Tribune*, 27 May 1918; "T. R. and Taft in Long Chat," *New York Sun*, 27 May 1918; Taft to Katherine Wulsin, 4 July 1918, in Ness, "Taft and the Great War," p. 19; Roosevelt to Albert J. Beveridge, 31 October 1918, Roosevelt Papers.

34. "Change in Congress Needed, Says Taft," *New York Times*, 20 July 1918.

35. William Howard Taft, "Wilson's Dialectic," 10 October 1918, in Vivian, ed., *Taft: Collected Editorials*, p. 100; Taft to Horace Taft, 15 October 1918, WHT.

36. "An Appeal for a Democratic Congress," 19 October 1918, in Arthur S. Link et al., eds., *The Papers of Woodrow Wilson*, vol. 51, *September 14–November 8, 1918* (Princeton, N.J.: Princeton University Press, 1985), p. 382.

37. Taft to Charles P. Taft, 27 October 1918, WHT; "Return Republican Congress Next Tuesday, Taft Urges," *Los Angeles Times*, 2 November 1918.

38. Charles D. Hilles to Taft, 28 October 1918, WHT. For other praise for Taft's stance, see Bernard Moses to Taft, 28 October 1918, WHT; Luther A. Brewer to Taft, 30 October 1918, WHT. For the Roosevelt-Taft statement, see "T.R. and Taft Plead," *Washington Post*, 1 November 1918.

39. Roosevelt to Taft, 15 August 1918, 26 August 1918, Roosevelt Papers; Roosevelt to Beveridge, 31 October 1918, Roosevelt Papers.

40. Isaac Ullman to Taft, 16 November 1918, WHT; Taft to Katherine Wulsin, 7 December 1918, in Ness, "Taft and the Great War," p. 21.

41. F. F. Van de Water, "Roosevelt Rests with Flag He Loved; Nation's Leaders Mourn at Grave," *New York Tribune*, 9 January 1918.

42. Taft to Helen Taft, 9 January 1919, WHT; Van de Water, "Roosevelt Rests with Flag He Loved," *New York Tribune*.

43. Henry F. Pringle, *The Life and Times of William Howard Taft*, 2 vols. (New York: Farrar & Rinehart, 1939), vol. 2, pp. 913–914.

44. "Brilliant Personality Gone (T. R.)," in Vivian, ed., *Taft: Collected Editorials*, p. 154.

CHAPTER 6. THE LEAGUE OR THE PARTY

1. Taft to Edward Bok, 29 January 1919, William Howard Taft Papers, Manuscript Division, Library of Congress (hereafter cited as WHT). "Enforce Prohibition," in James F. Vivian, ed., *William Howard Taft: Collected Editorials, 1917–1921* (New York: Praeger, 1990), p. 172.

2. Taft to Henry C. Coe, 14 November 1916, WHT; Taft to Gus Karger, 22 February 1919, WHT.

3. "Ask Taft to Act as Baseball Head," *New York Times*, 24 November 1918.

4. Michael T. Lynch, *Harry Frazee, Ban Johnson, and the Feud That Nearly Destroyed the American League* (Jefferson, N.C.: MacFarland, 2008), p. 55.

5. William C. Widenor, *Henry Cabot Lodge and the Search for an American Foreign Policy* (Berkeley, Calif.: University of California Press, 1980), p. 208; Henry Cabot Lodge to William Allen White, 16 November 1908, William Allen White Papers, Manuscript Division, Library of Congress; Hiram Johnson to Hiram Johnson Jr. and Archibald W. Johnson, 6 April 1917, in Robert E. Burke, ed., *The Diary Letters of Hiram Johnson*, 7 vols. (New York: Garland, 1983). There is no pagination for this series and letters can only be cited by date.

6. Albert W. Fox, "Wilson Is to Sail Early in December," *Washington Post*, 19 November 1918.

7. "Marshall's Duty to Assume Power," *Washington Post*, 27 November 1918; "Debate Wilson Trip," *Washington Post*, 4 December 1918. Sherman added that foreign influences had often shaped events. "The kiss of a sensuous woman has been known to change the history of nations."

8. William Howard Taft, "Wilson's Voyage Breaks No Law," and "The President's Trip," in Vivian, ed., *Taft: Collected Editorials*, pp. 121, 123, 131–133; Newton D. Baker to Woodrow Wilson, 5 December 1918, in Arthur S. Link et al., eds, *The Papers of Woodrow Wilson*, vol. 53, *November 9, 1918–January 11, 1919* (Princeton, N.J.: Princeton University Press, 1986), p. 323.

9. Taft to Katherine Wulsin, 7 December 1918, in Gary Ness, ed., "William Howard Taft and the Great War," *Cincinnati Historical Society Bulletin* 34 (1976): pp. 21–22; Taft to Jasper Thompson, 23 December 1918, WHT.

10. Wilson to Richard Hooker, 29 November 1918, Diary of Josephus Daniels, 19 November 1918, "A Statement," 18 December 1918, all in Link, *The Papers of Woodrow Wilson*, vol. 53, pp. 135, 243–244, 420.

11. William Howard Taft, "The League of Nations, What It Means and Why It Must Be," *National Geographic Magazine* 35 (January 1919): p. 66. See also William Howard Taft, "Problems for World Peace: The Questions That Confront an International Congress," *Forum* 61 (January 1919): p. 53. The campaign of the League to Enforce Peace is described in Ruhl J. Bartlett, *The League to Enforce Peace* (Chapel Hill: University of North Carolina Press, 1944), pp. 114–116.

12. "William Howard Taft Says Public Mind Favors League," *Washington Post*, 23 February 1919. This column, from the *Philadelphia Public Ledger*, is not included in James Vivian's edition of Taft's editorials.

13. Borah is quoted in John Milton Cooper, *Breaking the Heart of the World: Woodrow Wilson and the Fight for the League of Nations* (New York: Cambridge University Press, 2001), p. 57.

14. William Howard Taft, "The League Covenant," 17 February 1919, in Vivian, ed., *Taft: Collected Editorials*, pp. 177–178; "Taft Challenges League Opponents," *New York Times*, 26 February 1919.

15. Taft to Gus Karger, 22 February 1919, WHT. The senators to when Taft referred that have not previously been mentioned were James Reed, a Missouri Democrat who hated Wilson; Miles Poindexter, a Republican from Washington State; Frederick Hale, a Maine Republican; and Albert B. Fall of New Mexico, a Republican with whom Taft had clashed during his presidency.

16. Taft to Karger, 22 February 1919, WHT.

17. Taft to Wilson, 28 February 1918, WHT.

18. "Taft and Wilson Enter Big Meeting Arm in Arm," *New-York Tribune*, 5 March 1919.

19. "The League of Nations: Its Supporters, Its Opponents, and an Editorial Interpretation," *Outlook*, 12 March 1919, p. 421; William Howard Taft, "The Paris Covenant for a League of Nations 2," 4 March 1919, in Frank X. Gerrity, ed., *The Collected Works of William Howard Taft*: vol. 7, *Taft Papers on the League of Nations* (Athens: Ohio University Press, 2003), pp. 241–254.

20. Gerrity, ed., "The Paris Covenant," pp. 248, 253–254.

21. Ibid., p. 254; Taft to Robert A. Taft, 17 March 1919, WHT.

22. Cooper, *Breaking the Heart of the World*, pp. 55–57, is excellent on the circumstances of the introduction of the Round Robin.

23. Joseph P. Tumulty to Wilson, 16 March 1919, in Arthur S. Link et al., eds., *The Papers of Woodrow Wilson*, vol. 55, *February 8–March 16, 1919* (Princeton, N.J.: Princeton University Press, 1986), p. 540, conveying Taft's request; Cooper, *Breaking the Heart of the World*, p. 70.

24. "Taft Split Up the League to Enforce Peace," *New York Sun*, 18 March 1919; "Peace League Says There Is No Split," *New York Times*, 19 March 1919.

25. For Taft's suggestions, see "From William Howard Taft," 18 March 1919, 21 March 1919, 28 March 1919, 29 March 1919, in Link, *The Papers of Woodrow Wilson*, vol. 56, pp. 83, 157–159, 398–399, 485; Oscar Straus to Wilson, 17 April 1919, conveying message from Taft, in Link, *The Papers of Woodrow Wilson*, vol. 57, *April 5–22, 1919* (Princeton, N. J.: Princeton University Press, 1987), p. 445.

26. Cooper, *Breaking the Heart of the World*, p. 103, quotes Brandegee; Henry Cabot Lodge to Henry White, 8 April 1919, in Allan Nevins, *Henry White: Thirty Years of American Diplomacy* (New York: Harper & Bros, 1930), p. 413.

27. "As Borah Sees Taft," *Kansas City Star*, 7 June 1919.

28. Taft to Edward E. Whiting, 5 May 1919, WHT.

29. Taft to Horace Taft, 10 May 1919, WHT.

30. "Has Taft Lost His Stabilizer?" *Fort Wayne News and Sentinel*, 17 June 1919.

31. Lodge to Henry White, 2 July 1919, in Nevins, *Henry White*, p. 455.

32. From William Howard Taft, 28 June 1919, in Arthur S. Link, et al., eds., *The Papers of Woodrow Wilson*, vol. 61, *June 18–July 25, 1919* (Princeton, N. J.: Princeton University Press, 1989), p. 353.

33. Hilles to Taft, 11 July 1919, WHT.

34. Taft to Helen Taft, 23 June 1919, WHT.

35. Henry Taft to Taft, 9 July 1919, WHT; Taft to Karger, 17 July 1919, WHT.

36. "Substance of Taft's Proposed Interpretations to the Covenant of the League of Nations," *New York Times*, 24 July 1919.

37. "Taft, Urging Interpretations to Insure Ratification of League, Raps Wilson Policy," *New York Times*, 24 July 1919. See also Albert Poe, "League Compromise Suggested by Taft," *Washington Post*, 24 July 1919; "Taft in Treaty Plea to Democrats," *Evening World* [New York], 24 July 1919.

38. "Taft, Urging Interpretations to Insure Ratification."

39. William Wiseman to Arthur Balfour, 18 July 1919, in E. L. Woodward and Rohan Butler, eds., *Documents on British Foreign Policy, 1919–1939: First Series*, vol. 5 (London: Her Majesty's Stationery Office, 1954), p. 984; Karger to Taft, 19 July 1919, WHT.

40. "The Political Squalls Attending Peace-Making," *Burlington Free Press and Times*, 31 July 1919.

41. "Reject Any Compromise: Opponents Say Taft Suggestions Don't Fill the Bill," *New York Times*, 25 July 1919.

42. David Lawrence, "Taft's Effort Causes Dismay at the White House; Shows Weakness," *Fort Worth Star Telegram*, 25 July 1919.

43. Newton D. Baker to Woodrow Wilson, 24 July 1919, in Arthur S. Link et al., eds., *The Papers of Woodrow Wilson*, vol. 61, *June 18–July 25, 1919*, p. 614.

44. Taft to LeBaron Colt, 24 July 1919, WHT; LeBaron Colt to Taft, 29 July 1919, WHT. Colt was a Republican senator from Rhode Island.

45. "Reject Any Compromise," *New York Times*, 25 July 1919; "Backs Taft's Stand Indorsing the League," *New York Times*, 1 August 1919.

46. Taft to Lowell, 27 July 1919, WHT; Lowell to Taft, 7 August 1919, WHT.

47. Taft to Short, 24 August 1919, WHT.

48. Bartlett, *The League to Enforce Peace*, pp. 149–150

CHAPTER 7. TAFT AND THE TREATY DEFEATED

1. Gus Karger to Taft, 24 July 1919, William Howard Taft Papers, Manuscript Division, Library of Congress (hereafter cited as WHT); "Taft's League Talk Ignored in the Senate," *New York Sun*, 29 August 1919.

2. "Today: Pretty Bubble," *Washington Times*, 28 July 1919.

3. "President," *Fort Wayne News and Sentinel*, 6 August 1919; "Will Hays, Mr. Taft," *Miami Herald*, 12 August 1919.

4. William C. Widenor, *Henry Cabot Lodge and the Search for an American Foreign Policy* (Berkeley: University of California Press, 1980), p. 235.

5. Henry Cabot Lodge to John T. Morse, 11 October 1912, Henry Cabot Lodge Papers, Massachusetts Historical Society, Boston (hereafter cited as Lodge Papers). Lodge to Theodore Roosevelt, 29 April 1909, in Henry Cabot Lodge, ed., *Selections from the Correspondence of Theodore Roosevelt and Henry Cabot Lodge, 1884–1918*, 2 vols. (New York: Charles Scribner's Sons, 1925), vol. 2, p. 334. Lodge to Roosevelt, 27 December 1909, Lodge Papers, offered Lodge's most sustained criticism of Taft's presidential performance. The senator omitted this important document from the edition of his correspondence with Roosevelt, perhaps because Taft was still alive.

6. Taft to Lodge, 22 February 1919, WHT.

7. Henry Cabot Lodge, *Treaty of Peace with Germany: Speech of Henry Cabot Lodge of Massachusetts in the Senate of the United States, Tuesday, August 12, 1919* (Washington, D.C.: Government Printing Office, 1919).

8. William Howard Taft, "Senator Lodge and the League," 27 August 1919, in James F. Vivian, ed., *William Howard Taft: Collected Editorials, 1917–1921* (New York: Praeger, 1990), pp. 261–269; Lodge to James T. Williams, 24 July 1919, Lodge Papers, quoted in John Milton Cooper, *Breaking the Heart of the World: Woodrow Wilson and the Fight for the League of Nations* (New York: Cambridge University Press, 2001), p. 132.

9. Taft to Edward E. Whiting, 12 September 1919, WHT.

10. "Taft Refuses Trip in Airplane," *Wilkes–Barre Times Leader*, 18 August 1919; "Taft Hits Plumb Plan," *New York Times*, 11 August 1919; Bill Price, "'Smiling Bill' Taft Mum on Gift from Carnegie, but Eats 'Three Squares' a Day While D.C. Applauds $10,000 Annuity as Patriotic Example," *Washing-*

ton Times, 1 September 1919. Taft to Margaret T. Corwin, 10 October 1919, WHT, discussed his course schedule for the fall semester at Yale and his resumed teaching duties.

11. Herbert F. Margulies, *The Mild Reservationists and the League of Nations in the Senate* (Columbia, Mo.: University of Missouri Press, 1989), pp. 79, 82, 83, is excellent on the provisions and significance of the Johnson amendment.

12. "Johnson Assails Wilson in Indiana," *New York Times*, 12 September 1919.

13. "Taft and Glass Plead for Budget," *New York Times*, 5 October 1919.

14. Taft to A. Lawrence Lowell, 5 October 1919, WHT.

15. Carter Field, "Reservation to Be Yielded by Democrats," *New-York Tribune*, 5 October 1919; Karger to Taft, 5 October 1919, WHT.

16. "Politics by the Occasional Prophet," *Washington Times*, 16 October 1919.

17. Col. Roosevelt's Ideals to Save U.S., Says Taft," *New-York Tribune*, 27 October 1919.

18. Ruhl J. Bartlett, *The League to Enforce Peace* (Chapel Hill, N.C.: University of North Carolina Press, 1944), p. 152; Cooper, *Breaking the Heart of the World*, p. 249.

19. Taft to William Starr Myers, 20 January 1920, WHT.

20. Taft to Horace Taft, 7 February 1920, WHT.

21. Taft to Horace Taft, 7 June 1920, WHT.

22. William Howard Taft, "Republican Frontrunners," 1 January 1920 in Vivian, ed., *Taft: Collected Editorials*, p. 330.

23. Ibid., p. 332; Taft to Henry W. Taft, 21 March 1920, WHT.

24. "Urge Treaty Parley," *Washington Post*, 24 November 1919; "For Treaty of Some Kind," *New York Times*, 1 December 1919.

25. Cooper, *Breaking the Heart of the World*, p. 289.

26. "Democrats Try to Mend Treaty with G.O.P. Aid," *Washington Herald*, 30 December 1919; "Taft Asserts His Hat Is Not 'In the Ring,'" *Washington Herald*, 24 January 1920.

27. McNary to Taft, 13 January 1920; Karger to Taft, 31 January 1920, WHT; Taft to Karger, January 21, 1920, WHT.

28. "Taft Confers with Mild Group," *New York Times*, 24 January 1920.

29. "Conferees on Treaty Break Finally; Lodge Rejects Plan on Article X; Fight To Be Reopened in Senate Feb. 10," *New York Times*, 31 January 1920.

30. Taft to W. Reginald Wheeler, 6 February 1920, WHT.

31. Ibid.

32. "Taft Defends Lansing; Says Public Is with Him," *Washington Post*, 15 February 1920.

33. Taft to John J. Spurgeon, 22 February 1920, WHT.

34. Taft to Henry W. Taft, 21 March 1920, WHT.

35. "Taft Asserts His Hat Is Not 'In the Ring,'" *Washington Herald*, 24 January 1920.

36. Taft to John J. Spurgeon, 26 February 1920, WHT.

37. "Miss Helen Taft, Dean of Bryn Mawr, To Wed," *New York Times*, 2 June 1920; "Miss Helen Taft Will Be Bride of Yale Instructor," *New York Evening World*, 2 June 1920; "Helen Taft Becomes Bride of F. J. Manning," *New-York Tribune*, 16 July 1920.

38. Taft to Helen Taft, 13 January 1920, in Ishbel Ross, *An American Family: The Tafts, 1678 to 1964* (Cleveland, Ohio: World Publishing Co., 1964), pp. 319, 320.

39. "Canada Asks Taft to Represent Her," *New York Times*, 15 June 1920.

40. Ibid.

41. "Harding and Coolidge Should Sweep Country Says Taft in Message," *Washington Post*, 13 June 1920.

42. Republican National Committee, *Republican Campaign Text-Book, 1920* (New York, 1920), pp. 19, 20.

43. William Howard Taft, "The Harding–Coolidge Ticket," 19 June 1920, in Vivian, ed., *Taft: Collected Editorials*, p. 425; Richard Coke Lower, *A Bloc of One: The Political Career of Hiram Johnson* (Stanford, Calif.: Stanford University Press, 1993), p. 144.

CHAPTER 8. AMBITION ACHIEVED

1. William Howard Taft to Robert McDougal, 26 September 1920, William Howard Taft Papers, Manuscript Division, Library of Congress (hereafter cited as WHT).

2. Taft to H. A. Powell, 17 October 1920, WHT.

3. U.S. Senate, "The League Covenant," 11 September 1919, *Congressional Record*, 66 Cong., 1st Sess. (Washington, D. C.: Government Printing Office, 1919), p. 5221.

4. Ibid., p. 5225.

5. Randolph C. Downes, *The Rise of Warren Gamaliel Harding, 1865–1920* (Columbus: Ohio State University Press, 1970), pp. 328, 331. Downes is excellent in his analysis of Harding's clever statements about the league and his appeals as a presidential candidate to nationalism and Americanism.

6. John Milton Cooper, *Breaking the Heart of the World: Woodrow Wilson and the Fight for the League of Nations* (New York: Cambridge University Press, 2001), p. 383.

7. William Howard Taft, "Harding's Acceptance," 30 July 1920, in James F. Vivian, ed., *William Howard Taft: Collected Editorials, 1917–1921* (New York: Praeger, 1990), p. 442.

8. Ibid., p. 441.

9. William Howard Taft, "Mr. Wilson and the Campaign," *Yale Review* 10 (October 1920): pp. 1–25.

10. Taft to Fred Winslow Adams, 30 July 1920, WHT.

11. John Callan O'Laughlin, "Taft's Hope Doomed," *Washington Post*, 1 August 1920.

12. Taft to Harold Stanley Pellard, 30 July 1920, WHT.

13. "Taft Hopes Harding Will Accept the League with Lodge Reservations," *Evening World*, 6 August 1920; "Taft Clashes with Harding on League," *New York Times*, 7 August 1920.

14. William Howard Taft, "A Personal Statement," 2 August 1920, in Vivian, ed., *Taft: Collected Editorials*, pp. 444–445.

15. Taft to William H. Short, 7 August 1920 (two letters), WHT.

16. Taft to Charles Robinson Smith, 2 August 1920, WHT; Taft to Charles D. Norton, 19 August 1920, WHT.

17. "Harding Men Aim to Shift League as Main Issue," *New York Times*, 11 August 1920.

18. James M. Cox to Wilson, 27 September 1920, William G. McAdoo to Wilson, Wilson to McAdoo, 4 October 1920, in Arthur S. Link et al., eds. *The Pa-*

pers of Woodrow Wilson, vol. 65 (Princeton, N.J.: Princeton University Press, 1992), pp. 159, 180–181, 184–185.

19. Robert T. Small, "Wilson Took Taft's Advice on Treaty." *Washington Post*, 11 October 1920. See also "League Changes Sought by Taft Were All Made," *Evening World*, 11 October 1920.

20. "League Changes at His Request Admitted by Taft," *Evening World*, 11 October 1920; Karger to Taft, 12 October 1920, WHT.

21. Karger to Taft, 16 October 1920, WHT.

22. "Harding Rejects the League Outright; Wants Troops Back after Peace Vote; Cox Accepts Issue Says 'I'm for League,'" *New York Times*, 8 October 1920. Taft to Mischler, 12 October 1920, WHT.

23. Taft to H. A. Powell, 17 October 1920, WHT; Taft issued a lengthy statement defending Harding's approach to the league on 16 October 1920, WHT; "Taft Thinks League Safe," *New York Times*, 20 October 1920.

24. Richard Hooker to Taft, 21 October 1920, WHT.

25. Taft to Hooker, 1 November 1920, WHT.

26. Taft to Warren G. Harding, 3 November 1920, WHT.

27. Taft to Harry M. Daugherty, 20 October 1920, WHT.

28. Harding to Taft, 5 November 1920, WHT; "Predict Taft Will Be Chief Justice," *Washington Times*, 8 November 1920.

29. William Howard Taft, "The Progressive World Struggle of the Jews for Civil Equality," *National Geographic Magazine* 36 (July 1919): pp. 1–23.

30. "Taft Denounces Attacks on Jews," *Washington Post*, 24 December 1920. Taft was also a signatory of a letter signed by many prominent Christians, including President Wilson, denouncing anti-Semitism. See letter from John Spargo, with enclosure, 22 December 1920, in Link, ed., *Papers of Woodrow Wilson*, vol. 65, pp. 540–542.

31. Taft to Helen Taft, 26 December 1920, WHT.

32. Ibid.

33. Ibid.

34. Ibid.

35. "Harding's League Ideas Please Taft," *Washington Post*, 25 December 1920.

36. Taft to Helen Taft, 26 December 1920, WHT; Karger to Taft, 14 January 1921, WHT.

37. "Taft Selected as Chief Justice of Supreme Court," *New York Times*, 29 March 1921. Beyond its bare assertion of the likelihood that Taft would be appointed, the article was rather light on actual facts. Taft to Henry Sloan Coffin, 5 April 1921, WHT.

38. Taft to Harry Daugherty, 11 April 1921, WHT.

39. Taft to C. Sidney Shepard, 11 April 1921, WHT; for Harding's inaugural statement, see George C. Herring, *From Colony to Superpower: U.S. Foreign Relations Since 1776* (New York: Oxford University Press, 2008), p. 450.

40. Draft statement, 8 May 1921, WHT; "A Budget At Last," May 30, 1921, in Vivian, ed., *Taft: Collected Editorials*, pp. 582–583.

41. Taft to Shepard, 11 April 1921, WHT.

42. "Chief Justice White," 20 May 1921, in Vivian, *Taft: Collected Editorials*, p. 581.

43. Frank Brandegee to Taft, 14 June 1921, WHT; Karger to Taft, 14 June 1921, 21 June 1921, WHT.

44. "Ex-President Taft Succeeds White as Chief Justice," *New York Times*, 1 July 1921; "Harding Appoints Taft Chief Justice; Senate Confirms Him, 61 to 4," *New-York Tribune*, 1 July 1921.

45. "Taft Chuckles with Delight," *New York Times*, 1 July 1921; Karger to Taft, 30 June 1921, WHT.

46. "Harding Appoints Taft Chief Justice; Senate Confirms Him 61 to 4," *New-York Tribune*, 1 July 1921. George F. Sparks, ed., *A Many-Colored Toga: The Diary of Henry Fountain Ashurst* (Tucson: University of Arizona Press, 1962), pp. 147–148, recorded one senator's view of the debate about Taft.

47. Willis Fletcher Johnson, "Affairs of the World," *North American Review* 214 (September 1921): p. 418; "Chief Justice Taft," *Washington Post*, 2 July 1921; Samuel Spring, "Two Chief Justices: Edward Douglass White and William Howard Taft," *American Review of Reviews* 64 (August 1921): p. 162.

48. "The Chief Justice—A Mistaken Appointment," *Nation* 113 (July 1921): p. 32.

49. Fanny Edwards to Taft, 30 June 1921, WHT; John H. Finley to Taft, 1 July 1921, WHT; S. L. Calhoun to Taft, 1 July 1921.

50. Charles W. Duke, "Taft, the Greatest of Globe Trotters for Humanity: New Chief Justice Noted as the Most Traveled Man in Public Life," *Washington Herald Magazine of Features and Fiction*, 17 July 1921.

A NOTE ON SOURCES

This note is designed to provide comments on the most useful sources for this study. It is not meant to be an exhaustive collection of everything relevant to Taft's life between 1913 and 1921.

The main sources for a study of William Howard Taft between 1913 and 1921 are the former president's personal papers at the Library of Congress. Microfilmed, indexed, and easy to use, the Taft Papers provide a full record of events from his perspective. They reveal, for example, his role in the construction of the Lincoln Memorial, his interest in policy toward the Philippines, and his involvement with the League to Enforce Peace. The letters from his Washington correspondent, newspaper reporter Gus Karger, are especially valuable. Gary Ness, ed., "William Howard Taft and the Great War," *Cincinnati Historical Society Bulletin* 34 (1976): pp. 6–23, provided letters that Taft wrote to a friend in Paris during World War I.

Other manuscript sources were helpful on specific points. The Mabel Boardman Papers at the Library of Congress; the Winthrop Murray Crane Papers at the Massachusetts Historical Society; the Will H. Hays Papers at the Lilly Library, Indiana University; and the Theodore Roosevelt Papers in the Library of Congress were indispensable. The relevant volumes of Arthur S. Link et al., eds, *The Papers of Woodrow Wilson* (Princeton, N.J.: Princeton University Press, 1978–1994) were vital for understanding the Taft-Wilson relationship. Clarence Wunderlin et al., *The Papers of Robert A. Taft, Volume 1, 1889–1939* (Kent, Ohio: Kent State University Press, 1997), conveys a good deal of pertinent information about the elder Taft.

Taft wrote at great length on a variety of subjects during this period. Paulo E. Coletta, ed., *William Howard Taft: A Bibliography* (Westport, Conn.: Meckler, 1989), is a convenient guide to Taft's many publications. Frank X. Gerrity, ed., *The Collected Works of William Howard Taft: Taft Papers on the League of Nations* (Athens: Ohio University Press, 2003), is a good compilation of Taft's writings about his campaign to secure adoption of the League of Nations in the United States. James F. Vivian, ed., *William Howard Taft: Collected Editorials, 1917–1921* (Westport, Conn.: Prager, 1990), is a valuable collection of Taft's journalistic opinions during a crucial period of World War I and its aftermath.

Taft remained a favorite subject for reporters throughout this period. In addition to such standbys as the *New York Times* and the *Washington Post,* the ability to access newspapers from around the country through the "Chronicling America" website of the Library of Congress allowed for a much more thorough survey of Taft's activities.

Biographies of Taft were of only modest value for this period. Henry F. Pringle, *The Life and Times of William Howard Taft,* 2 vols., (New York: Farrar & Rinehart, 1939), is badly dated and skimpy in its coverage of key events during this phase of Taft's life. Judith Icke Anderson, *William Howard Taft: An Intimate History* (New York: W. W. Norton, 1981), focused on the presidency. William Manners, *TR & Will: A Friendship That Split the Republican Party* (New York: Harcourt, Brace & World, 1969), has only a brief chapter on the two men after the Taft presidency. Frederick C. Hicks, *William Howard Taft: Yale Professor of Law & New Haven Citizen* (New Haven, Conn.: Yale University Press, 1945), has much helpful information on Taft's academic career.

On specific issues that involved Taft, Christopher A. Thomas, *The Lincoln Memorial & American Life* (Princeton, N.J.: Princeton University Press, 2002) is thorough and informative about Taft's participation. Julia F. Irwin, *Making the World Safe: The American Red Cross and a Nation's Humanitarian Awakening* (New York: Oxford University Press, 2013), illuminates Taft's key role in the working of the organization. Marian Moser Jones, *The American Red Cross from Clara Barton to the New Deal* (Baltimore, Md.: Johns Hopkins University Press, 2013), also explores Taft's involvement with the fate of Mabel Boardman and her organization.

More research needs to be done on Taft's participation in the affairs of the American Bar Association. Jerold S. Auerbach, *Unequal Justice: Lawyers and Social Change in Modern America* (New York: Oxford University Press, 1976) provides an indication of the major issues regarding the ABA.

For the National War Labor Board, Valerie Jean Connor, *The National War Labor Board: Stability, Social Justice, and the Voluntary State in World War I* (Chapel Hill: University of North Carolina Press, 1983) yields much, with careful reading, on Taft's leadership of the panel. Joseph A. McCartin, *Labor's Great War: The Struggle for Industrial Democracy and the Origins of Modern American Labor Relations, 1912–1921* (Chapel Hill: University of North Carolina Press, 1997), focuses on Taft in more detail. Maria Eucharia Meehan, "Frank P. Walsh and the American Labor Movement" (PhD diss., New York University, 1962) has important information on Walsh's collaborative efforts with Taft.

The debate between the former president and the Wilson administration about the future of the Philippines can be traced in Francis Burton Harrison, *The Corner-Stone of Philippine Independence: A Narrative of Seven Years* (New York: The Century Co., 1922), which is very critical of Taft, and Peter W. Stanley, *A Nation in the Making: The Philippines and the United States,*

1899–1921 (Cambridge, Mass.: Harvard University Press, 1974) which is sympathetic to Harrison and the Wilson administration.

For Taft and the fight over the confirmation of Louis D. Brandeis to the Supreme Court, the two essential accounts are A. L. Todd, *Justice on Trial: The Case of Louis D. Brandeis* (New York: McGraw-Hill, 1964), and Melvin I. Urofsky, *Louis D. Brandeis: A Life* (New York: Pantheon, 2009). Important background information is in Alexander M. Bickel and Benno C. Schmidt Jr., *The Oliver Wendell Holmes Devise History of the Supreme Court of the United States,* vol. 9, *The Judiciary and Responsible Government, 1910–1921* (New York: Macmillan, 1984).

The literature on the League to Enforce Peace and Taft's campaign for the League of Nations is voluminous. League to Enforce Peace, *Enforced Peace: Proceedings of the First Annual National Assemblage of the League to Enforce Peace, Washington, May 26–27, 1916* (Washington, D.C.: League to Enforce Peace, 1916), recounts the first national gathering of the league and includes Taft's important speech. Ruhl J. Bartlett, *The League to Enforce Peace* (Chapel Hill: University of North Carolina Press, 1944), is the standard work, but a new history of that organization, in light of modern work on the League of Nations, would be desirable. The background of Taft's thinking on arbitration, war, and peace issues is much discussed in David S. Patterson, *Toward a Warless World: The Travail of the American Peace Movement, 1887–1914* (Bloomington: Indiana University Press, 1976). Herbert F. Margulies, *The Mild Reservationists and the League of Nations Controversy in the Senate* (Columbia: University of Missouri Press, 1989), has much of interest on Taft, who was, in effect, a leading mild reservationist outside of the Senate.

For a general treatment of the League fight, I relied on the excellent book by John Milton Cooper Jr., *Breaking the Heart of the World: Woodrow Wilson and the Fight for the League of Nations* (New York: Cambridge University Press, 2001). William C. Widenor, *Henry Cabot Lodge and the Search for an American Foreign Policy* (Berkeley: University of California Press, 1980), shed helpful light on the policy tensions between Taft and the Massachusetts senator. Also very informative for Taft's participation in the league controversy are Warren F. Kuehl, *Seeking World Order: The United States and International Organization to 1920* (Nashville, Tenn.: Vanderbilt University Press, 1969), and Thomas J. Knock, *To End All Wars: Woodrow Wilson and the Quest for a New World Order* (Princeton, N.J.: Princeton University Press, 1992).

For important aspects of Taft's personal life, Philippe Dube, *Charlevoix: Two Centuries at Murray Bay* (Kingston & Montreal: McGill-Queen's University Press, 1990), is informative on his summer home in Canada. Carl Sferrazza Anthony, *Nellie Taft: The Unconventional First Lady of the Ragtime Era* (New York: William Morrow, 2005), looks at how the Tafts lived in New Haven and Washington from 1913 to 1921.

INDEX